Ordering Information
Special discounts are available on quantity purchases by corporations, associations, and others. For details, contact the publisher at the address below.
Hello@BlackSheepLibrary.com

Publisher's Cataloging-in-Publication Data
Emma Stevens, *Choosing to Breathe*

Cover photograph by Eileen Skahill
Cover design by Kara Rubinstein Deyerin

ISBN 978-1-967021-98-7 (Hardback)
ISBN 978-1-967021-99-4 (Paperback)
ISBN 978-1-967021-97-0 (eBook)

Copyright © 2025
Black Sheep Library, LLC
PO Box 86
Maple Valley, WA 98038
USA

Praise for Choosing to Breathe

"In Emma Steven's third book, *Choosing to Breathe*, she continues the journey toward wholeness, healing and embracing life despite childhood trauma and adulthood struggles. Emma traces many of her challenges back to being relinquished soon after birth by her mother, and adopted by alcoholic parents. She and her adoptive brother, although raised by the same parents in the same household, never talked about their adoption or the abuse they endured. As an adult, Emma chooses to embrace therapy, healing and forgiveness while caring for her aging adoptive parents. Through creative imagining, she creates and nurtures the wounded younger parts of herself, bringing disparate pieces together into a whole. *Choosing to Breathe* is inspiring, and is a testament to embracing life deeply, even in the wake of deep trauma."

—Diane Shifflett

"Anyone who spent a childhood living in service to the big people in their lives will appreciate how Emma

Stevens reclaims herSelf. *Choosing to Breathe* shares how, from selves that were fractured in order to be valued, Emma found wholeness. We all can."

—Lori Holden

"Emma describes the most traumatized parts of herself with such genuine affection, and connects with them so endearingly, you can't help but feel inspired. Through the relationships she forms with these wounded, scared parts and the trust she builds with them, she gives hope that it's possible not only to heal our deepest wounds but also to transcend them. It gives you a sense of magic."

—Kathy Mackechney, LCSW, Certified IFS Therapist and Approved Consultant

"Emma Stevens has done it again! In *Choosing to Breathe*, she masterfully uses her own story to illuminate the often-abstract concept of IFS/Parts Therapy. As an adoptee who's been urged to try it, this book finally made it click! One of my favorite authors offers readers a memorable and profound exploration of trauma, resilience, and the power of breath, much like James Nestor's *Breath*. A must-read for hyper-vigilant adoptees seeking to calm their nervous systems and for therapists looking for a relatable way to explain Parts Work."

—Rebecca Autumn Sansom Filmmaker of *Reckoning with The Primal Wound*

For My Children

Acknowledgements

A significant reason for writing this final memoir is the influence of the people I've met since my first book, *The Gathering Place: An Adoptee's Story*, and my second book, *A Fire Is Coming*. Both books have set my life on a path to discovering individuals I would never have encountered otherwise. These individuals have enriched my life; however, I have also engaged with those who affirm my decision to maintain healthy boundaries. I've realized I need both types of relationships, but for different reasons. The common thread is that they have all helped me become more of the person I want to be.

Kathy Mackechney, LCSW, is both an adoptee and a certified Internal Family Systems (IFS) therapist who contributed a chapter in *Altogether US: Integrating the IFS Model with Key Modalities, Communities, and Trends*, by Jenna Riemersma, LPC. Kathy's chapter, "IFS and Adoptees: Healing Parts Burdened by Relinquishment Trauma," presents the idea that "Not All Parts Get Adopted." Her theory resonated with me, prompting me to uncover many truths about my own *parts*—both adopted and not adopted. Thank you, Kathy Mackechney, for sharing this concept and bringing it to my conscious awareness and to others.

As an adoptee who never found a mentor dedicated solely to uplifting me, I express my heartfelt gratitude to adoptee, author, and writing coach Anne Heffron. In her book, *You Don't Look Adopted*, she poignantly describes her life as an adoptee and grants us all permission to do the same through her memoir and other writings. I give a lot of credit to Anne for helping me write my books, thanks to her unwavering support and inspiration.

I am incredibly grateful for another adoptee who has accompanied me throughout my memoir journey: my editor, Diane Shifflett. Diane has demonstrated that an editor can also be a friend, offering a fresh perspective that leads to greater clarity. Her thoughtful and meticulous editing has not only improved the content of my writing but has also helped make it a beautiful experience.

Without my adult daughter by my side to help me navigate the final years of her grandparents' lives in their own home, I could not have accomplished this alone. Her steadfastness in helping me care for them while simultaneously completing her doctoral program was impressive. Words cannot express my love and gratitude for her, and I feel incredibly fortunate to have her in my life. I am also thankful for my son, whom I love dearly and wouldn't want to do life without.

A special thank you goes to my publisher, Kara Rubinstein Deyerin of Black Sheep Library, LLC. Kara's unique insight into the complexities of adoption, identity, and family dynamics and secrets has added more depth and color to *Choosing to Breathe*.

A poignant contrast in my life has been my relationships with therapists. I have encountered a dangerous sociopath, as well as two exceptional therapists who have been incredibly supportive. I am grateful for both experiences, despite narrowly escaping the former. When appropriately conducted by ethical, competent, kind, and caring counselors, therapy can help you find freedom.

And to all my parts: I see you, I feel you, I hear you, and I love you. Thank you for allowing me to update you and collaborate to make life smoother. I am grateful to each of you for the love and protection you have tirelessly provided in the best ways you knew. You are brilliant!

~Emma Stevens, aka Linda Pevac

Contents

"In the social jungle of human existence, there is no feeling of being alive without a sense of identity."

—**Erik Erikson**, *German Psychoanalyst*

"Parts are little inner beings who are trying their best to keep you safe."

—**Richard C. Schwartz**, *No Bad Parts: Healing Trauma and Restoring Wholeness with the Internal Family Systems Model*

Preface

Sinking my roots deeper and broader helps draw my mind closer to my heart. Conversely, living my life with a mind, body, and spirit that doesn't pursue radical awareness and acceptance can lead to regret and enduring, oppressive despair. It took decades of exploration for me to find a way out of ruminating on and reliving my trauma as if it were my identity.

In my first book, *The Gathering Place: An Adoptee's Story,* I connect with the younger parts of myself that were not seen, celebrated, loved, or nurtured. To adapt to my environment, aspects of my personality formed as a means of protection. When our parents cannot see us, we cannot fully see ourselves. The Gathering Place is a mythical and magical realm, allowing me to create a safe, healing space in my mind's eye, complete with a vivid green hill featuring a majestic oak tree and rope-and-wood bench swing. Here, I invite the younger versions of myself to join me for meaningful conversations and to begin the healing process for old wounds.

As an infant who endured the trauma of being separated from my first mother and relinquished at birth, I spent three months in an unknown foster home, waiting to be adopted. Ultimately, I was placed with adoptive parents and a family who were uneducated and unwilling to research the specialized needs that an adopted child requires to thrive. These early experiences placed my life on rocky terrain, where cultivating and sustaining healthy personal development proved difficult.

From that moment on, it felt as if I had become a shallow breather, anticipating my first mother's return. A sense of deprivation of my basic needs settled upon me.

It became clear to me, however, that I could not keep ruminating on my past, knowing that I would sink into the despair so prevalent in our society—not only experiencing personal sorrow but also living in a world that is ablaze. The tears of everything. Of the world. With unjust societies, humanitarian disasters, and ecological crises flickering around us, it is easy to feel hopeless, helpless, and overwhelmed.

Establishing The Gathering Place has helped me find my footing and rekindle my inherent creativity and curiosity, allowing me to first love myself so that I can then love others.

In my second book, *A Fire Is Coming*, I aimed to raise awareness about how relinquishment and adoption have influenced my life, as well as the mental and sexual exploitation I suffered at the hands of a mental health professional who was supposed to help and protect me. My book depicts a time when my mind, body, and spirit were on fire. This type of abuse by therapists, counselors, and doctors often goes unreported and, as a result, remains unaddressed by ethical governing boards and the judicial system. Adoptees are particularly vulnerable and susceptible to harm from mental health professionals who fail to prioritize their clients' needs by upholding the Hippocratic Oath to "do no harm." While vulnerability and openness are essential for effective therapy, adoptees frequently grapple with more profound trauma, unhealthy relationships with authority figures, trust issues, and identity struggles.

Many adoptees were relinquished at birth, which leads to early developmental trauma. Research indicates that the earlier the trauma—especially pre-verbal—the more challenging it is to access and repair the damage. The secondary trauma arises from being adopted into a family of strangers who do not biologically share the adoptee's innate qualities and temperament. In therapy, some adoptees need to be regressed to a childlike state, returning to the time of the trauma, to rewire their brains and emotions with the hope of integrating those early traumatic experiences to resolve them more healthily. The hope is that this deep work can reduce future struggles.

A therapist working with an adoptee has an obligation and responsibility to recognize their exceptionally vulnerable state and to educate themselves on the specific needs and challenges of living as an adopted person. In my adoptee community, it's widely agreed that those seeking counseling should primarily look for adoptee-competent therapists—professionals dedicated to and trained in trauma-informed care. If care and discernment are lacking when interviewing and selecting a therapist, one may experience more persistent issues than they did before starting the process.

As the author of *The Gathering Place* and *A Fire Is Coming*, I hoped to embark on a more prophetic journey where I've come to understand that everything in life belongs and is interconnected. The contrasts in life can teach us about the broader spectrum of experiences and perspectives, guiding us toward a more non-dualistic mindset—one where I can choose not to view things in black and white but rather appreciate the magnificent yet often complex relationships and connections among all things.

This new way of thinking also led me to understand, as I've heard the Hungarian-Canadian author Dr. Gabor Maté say, that life wanted me. Life wants life. This revelation opened my mind to the understanding that the universe *wanted* me. The proof is that I am here. Regardless of who my biological or adoptive family were and are, it's a miracle I was born—just as it is for any of us. Telling myself a story about being unwanted and not being "good enough" for my first mother to stay is something I'm challenging and now see as nothing more than a broken, false narrative.

What I didn't have as a child, but do have now,

is choice. I actively and continually confront my core issues, which I've heard Gabor Maté refer to as "not enoughness." I am dedicated to staying open and willing to replace and repair my self-deprecating and divisive thoughts with acceptance, love, and grace. I understand that transformation is not about perfection; instead, it's about becoming more human. This contemplative, meditative mindset, among other things, has begun to set me free.

One of the most remarkable aspects of *The Gathering Place* is that we can all create our own magical spaces to foster our growth and expansion. The act of revisiting our younger selves to offer comfort and repair helps them feel seen and heard. It may be the first time they have been asked how they feel. When we honor and thank these parts for helping us navigate our childhood difficulties, we begin to resolve old wounds and traumas. This is true because I've heard from adopted and non-adopted individuals who shared this after reading *The Gathering Place*. Creating a space for ourselves where love, patience, understanding, and grace abound is one of the most "self-honoring" gifts I've ever received. I invite you to join me as I return to The Gathering Place, continue to be transformed by this fantastical home, and discover how life can flourish when we choose to breathe.

Introduction

It was spring again at The Gathering Place. I've returned many times since creating my safe space, and I continue to learn more about what my younger parts needed and wanted—and still do. These different parts make up the totality of who I am. I know some of them well, and I'm learning to spend more time with them to validate and understand them better. I absorb more of what my unconscious tries to share each time I visit. Being here this time, with spring's promise of new beginnings, assures me I am right where I want to be.

Ever since I decided to write a new story for myself, I've diligently dismantled and deconstructed the thick, fibrous layers of my conditioning. These are rooted not only in my childhood but also in living in a society that often promotes feelings of not enoughness. Advertisements and marketing bombard us, convincing us to become something different from what we are and to purchase more and more. Most of our culture believes that more is better, yet it is never enough.

Consumerism relies on our feelings of not enoughness and our inability to resist buying things we don't need. It's another term for fear of scarcity. Just as I found myself consumed by trauma and paralyzed with the fear of not getting a seat during the childhood game of musical chairs, I can see how this mindset could easily extend into other areas of a person's life. Instead, having a perspective that includes and embraces *abundance* can provide a feeling of satiation through truth, gratitude, and a connection to awe and wonder. Another definition of freedom.

My first encounter outside my mother's womb was the experience of being taken from her—permanently. At least until I painstakingly tracked her down 24 years later. However, the deprivation I felt as an infant must have been crushing. Where was my mother? The separation from her instilled in me a fear of being deprived of the very thing I needed most to survive and thrive. I know this to be true because I was there.

To challenge my feelings and core beliefs about not being enough and my fears of scarcity, I had to explore the possibility that this was not a true story. I asked myself some soul-searching questions, hoping they would increase my understanding. Were my implicit memories based on facts? Or were they merely what I perceived to be accurate as an infant without the capacity for higher reasoning? Although my infant self experienced this life event in one way, could I now update my younger self with the new insights I have learned since then?

Can I update and integrate my parts to find a deeper understanding and, in turn, greater wholeness?

I was open and willing to embark on this journey. I was ready to move from a state of order—the way I had always perceived myself and life—to disorder, dismantling, and examining everything I had ever believed to be true, and then to reorder, experiencing a rebirth, a new chapter, and an exercise toward wholeness.

I began my journey a few years ago in the safe place I created on the green grassy hill, with the rope-and-wood bench swing attached to a big, old oak tree. Through the practice of the psychotherapy modality of EMDR (Eye Movement Desensitization and Reprocessing), which is a proven method to recover from trauma and PTSD symptoms, I was able to create this magical place in my mind's eye. EMDR, carried out by my certified therapist, effectively helped me access and lessen the intensity and emotions associated with my trauma memories by stimulating my brain bilaterally—sometimes using alternating handheld pulsing sensors and other times by following a visual that required rapid eye movements from right to left. The method, created by Francine Shapiro, PhD, "recognizes that the brain stores normal and traumatic memories differently. Often, the brain stores trauma memories in a way that doesn't allow for healthy healing." EMDR helped me to reprocess these memories of adverse events and put a time stamp on them to realize none of them were happening to me in the present.

Creating a safe place that felt like coming home was essential to my success. What I uncovered during my many visits to The Gathering Place opened my heart and eyes to the possibility that I might be good enough after all.

~

I looked up from my seated perch under the old oak tree to see my five-year-old self, Tabitha, staring at me intently. Her name means "gracious." There's a lightness about her that seems to glow. I loved that she appeared just as I remembered her. Her long, light brown ponytail was tied with a blue ribbon, and she wore a navy-blue pinafore with matching shorts.

"I'm ascared," Tabitha said as she dug her sneakered feet into the soft, virgin green grass. "I wanna help, but I don't wanna lose Mommy and Daddy." Tabitha wiped her tear-filled eyes with the bottom of her apron-like top. "I been waiting for 'em to get real mad and spank me for how bad I am. But nothin's happened yet!"

I got to my feet and motioned for her to come close so I could wrap my arms around her. Her statement made me think she had been waiting for the other shoe to drop. I began reflecting on our last conversation at The Gathering Place and realized that her fondness for me, which helped her open up, also made her feel shamefully disloyal to her parents. *Our* parents.

That is precisely why I keep returning to The Gathering Place. Out of honor, love, and respect, I bring with me the updated data—all the truths I've discovered up to the present day—to offer hope and healing to my younger selves who endured an oppressive state of being to survive the trauma of my childhood. I accept that I can never change the past, but I can go back in my mind's eye to mend those parts, making them less likely to show up unannounced today with outdated thoughts, beliefs, and desires. Not to mention my effort to bring healing to the unattended wounds of my past. If I can be diligent in providing comfort and keep asking what they needed back then to not only feel safe but also seen and heard, then my present self has a much better chance of showing up whole in my life here and now.

"Hi, sweet Tabitha. I'm here, sweetheart. When you're ready, please tell me what's on your mind." I held her little body tightly as her tears began soaking through my cotton shirt.

As we rocked gently in the warm breeze, Tabitha leaned away from me and said, "I'm ascared they'll find out I like you and that you're my friend." Her face scrunched up with worry as if she had just seen a ghost.

Tabitha felt guilty for identifying with me and for feeling good about being nurtured by me. In her mind, anything that didn't glorify her adoptive parents as her saviors with absolute authority proved how "bad" she was. How disloyal she was. How disrespectful. Deserving of nothing.

Often, her parents withheld their love and affection to reinforce their disappointment in her. As a result, she felt a void—a hopeless sense of deprivation she had known since being relinquished at birth, caused by never being able to see her first mother again. This gutted, hollow feeling was too much for her to bear.

"Tabitha, what if I told you how brave I think you are? What if I told you how brilliant your strategies were in keeping us as safe as you did? And what if I told you how much I love you and how sorry I am that you're feeling this way?" I continued, "I'll return as much as necessary to remind you. Tabitha, what do you need from me right now?"

We sat down on the grassy ground. My weary five-year-old self leaned against me, her head resting on my shoulder, the weight of our two bodies merging felt like the warm, golden sun on my skin.

"I'm still ascared. What if Mommy and Daddy find me? Hurt me? And then I lose them? Why can't I be a good girl?" Tabitha climbed into my lap, and I cradled her like a baby.

"Sweetie," I said softly, taking my time. "I guided our parents through to the end—through their passing. And although they never recognized us for who we truly were or celebrated us, I feel good about having done so. We're now free to allow ourselves some rest. We can set aside the hypervigilance that kept us relatively safe before, but now hinders our way of being in the world. When they took their last breaths, I told them I loved them. I told them *we* loved them."

My adoptive parents passed away within six months of each other in 2022 and 2023. My older brother, Tim, died in 2020. The only ones who remember what happened in my childhood home are me and the parts of me that experienced it.

Tabitha's face contorted. "Where did they go?! I need to be with them! They're the only mommy and daddy I have!" she exclaimed.

"I understand, sweetie. I really do. I hope to help you see that I'm offering you a new way to view things and why you deserve to live freely now. I want to introduce you to a love that embraces all of you." I could feel Tabitha's panic. Her watery eyes began to spill tears down her cheeks. She grabbed my arm, and I felt her unexpected strength as she pleaded with me.

"Please, I need to go home now! Where are they? They'll find out I've been talking to you and I'll be in so much twouble!"

"It's **OK**, Tabitha. Shhh. I know you're scared. I want you to hear me say that you no longer have to live in fear. I'm here to protect you and provide the love you deserve."

"I want my mommy and daddy!" Tabitha buried her head in my lap.

The wild geese flew high above us in the clear blue air. Their honking echoed, gradually growing fainter as they headed toward unknown destinations.

Gazing at the densely forested hills beyond The Gathering Place, I asked, "Do you love your cat, Tabby?"

Tabby was our beloved furry companion from childhood. Her nature was as soft and nurturing as her multicolored fur and deep green eyes. She taught me what love meant and how to care for what I cherished.

Tabitha snapped out of her fear and grief, exclaiming, "I love her so much! She's the best kitty in the world!"

"Would you still love her even if she sometimes wants to be petted and loved by someone else? Would you call her a 'bad' kitty for wanting that? Would you withhold food, toys, and your love to make her feel guilty?"

I embraced all of myself, knowing Tabitha would need space and time to accept these new thoughts and beliefs. She would also need a lot of love, patience, and intentionality to embrace them as truth. Tabitha, my five-year-old self, had to recognize what true love looks like and what it does not. A grieving process had to unfold before a sustainable sense of peace could be achieved—something she never had the space or permission to grieve before. I was committed to embarking on this journey of expansion, not just for Tabitha and myself, but for all of me.

1

Self-Fulfilling Prophecies

"All right, friends, let's put away our pencils and paper. It's time for playtime! Who's up for some musical chairs today?" Mrs. Magoye, my kindergarten teacher, sang out as she held a 10-inch black vinyl record high in the air. The whole class responded with high-pitched cheers and loud clapping.

Everyone except me, that is. Musical chairs was never my favorite game. The thought of the music playing—and then suddenly stopping—sent a heart-pounding panic through my entire body. It was a fear so consuming that it left me no space to experience what was meant to be a fun game in any way other than as a trigger for my fight-or-flight response.

With the chairs arranged in a medium-sized circle, Mrs. Magoye gently lowered the record player needle onto the record, sending upbeat musical notes into the air of the kindergarten classroom.

That's when I felt my anxiety begin to accelerate

rapidly. With sweaty palms, I followed my classmates around the perimeter of the chairs as we listened to the lively music from the school's record player. Having played the game many times, I knew how it would unfold. We excitedly scooted in front of each chair and then paused, anticipating the screech of the record player needle suddenly lifted off the record.

"Keep moving, friends! The music is still playing!" My classmates and I listened and reluctantly began to move faster as instructed. It created a false sense of trust while maneuvering around those chairs—not knowing whether you'd end up in front of one when the music stopped. You were out if you didn't sit in a chair after the music ceased. The game would be over for you.

A musical rendition of "Pop Goes the Weasel" was playing. The game of Pop Goes the Weasel also has a frightening conclusion, with the sudden ejection of a puppet on a spring from a box. The tune was fitting for the game we were playing.

I thought, "It's been too long! Why hasn't the teacher lifted the needle yet?" Anticipating the music to stop, I held my breath to hear better the moment the teacher silenced the tune. I could feel sweat beading on my forehead, and a headache formed and throbbed between my furrowed brows.

The longer the music played, the more I thought about how scared I was and how it related to my childhood home life—the paralyzing uncertainty of what was coming next. My parents' sudden mood changes, erratic behaviors, and the need for my brother and me to walk on eggshells were the norm in our adoptive home. We had been adopted as infants and had learned of our adoption at a very young age. My brother and I are two and a half years apart. The difficulties stemmed from our adoptive parents' refusal to acknowledge that my brother and I had different biological backgrounds. I had always suspected their ignoring our past was their way of pretending it had never happened. If my parents could get my brother and me to ignore and deny our beginnings, they believed they could exert control over us, allowing them to pose as the omnipotent saviors they demanded we think them to be.

And it worked. I looked to my parents as the gods who allowed me to live with them, to have a bed and food, and to dictate and instill within me the insidious conditioning that had my psyche in a chokehold.

One wrong move, and I could be out. Abandoned. Just as I perceived my first mom doing when she walked out of my life on the day I was born, never to return, I felt my adoptive parents could do the same. As a result, I adapted, submitted, and conformed. I became a people-pleaser and a perfectionist who also developed an excessive sense of responsibility for carrying burdens that were never mine to bear—just to survive. Not to mention honing the skill of being able to read and respond to the ever-changing temperature in the room.

Safety. Trust. Achieving a home that embodied these values eluded my older brother, Tim, and me. The ability to simply be children instead of bearing the responsibility of caring for our parents' emotional needs was not possible. The internal anxiety and chaos that settled within me is what I now recognize as extreme hypervigilance. There seemed to be comfort in adopting this way of thinking.

Another life-sustaining strategy my young mind embraced was that of loving my captors, known as Stockholm Syndrome. The power imbalances my parents used to secure my compliance caused me to blur the lines between what a genuine, loving relationship resembles and what I had experienced. Instead, survival became my objective. I employed the tools I believed helped me achieve this: loving, submitting to, and placating them—all essential for my survival.

Screech. I noticed a bit too late that the music had stopped. Panic surged within me, and simultaneously, a harsh voice in my head yelled, *"You dummy! You missed it!"*

The boy next to me had stealthily maneuvered beside me, then behind me, and was now seated in what should have been my chair. He looked up at me as if he'd just swallowed a small bird.

Mrs. Magoye looked in my direction. "Oh, Emma! I'm so sorry! Please have a seat at the back of the room. You're out." Turning back to the remaining participants in the game, she exclaimed, "Congratulations, John! All right, let's start again."

Once again, the music of "Pop Goes the Weasel" started playing. My panic about playing the game transformed into an intense feeling of inadequacy, overwhelming loneliness, and emptiness. At that moment, I zoomed out from the room and saw myself below, slowly slinking to the back of the classroom while the rest of me hovered near the ceiling. I watched as tears welled in my eyes, then trickled down the front of my dress and splashed onto my black patent shoes. I noticed my little shoulders slump as I sank into a dark blue plastic chair, keeping my gaze fixed on the classroom floor.

My dissociated state, hovering above, protected the "me" I was viewing below. Although it was a creative coping strategy, I was—even at five years old—convinced that getting eliminated from the game was entirely my fault. If only I had been more alert, assertive, or intelligent. If only I had been good enough. Maybe then I would be loved enough to be worthy of not being excluded, exiled, or abandoned. Maybe then I could have a seat, too.

The conditioning of my mind, body, and spirit began in my mother's womb. She knew throughout her pregnancy that she was going to relinquish me. As a result, I swam in the waters of her angst and negativity surrounding her unfortunate pregnant condition. I absorbed her anxiety and regrets—instead of her love, longing, and desire to hold me close and cherish my face.

Feelings of inadequacy had taken root within me. I believed all the evidence was there—proof that I was unwanted and not good enough to stay for. Without examining these beliefs, I was destined to make this a lifelong self-fulfilling prophecy.

2

Athena

One day, on the grassy hill, I asked a young girl who'd joined me, "What's your name?" I tried to enunciate loudly to compete with The Gathering Place's brief gusts of wind.

She stared at me blankly, then tilted her head to the side. Although her hair suddenly blew across her cheeks, I could see the unmistakable crooked smile forming on her face.

With a gleam in her eye and a quick tuck of her light brown hair behind her ears, she playfully asked, "Who do *you* think I am, Emma?"

I paused before brightening as if a light had illuminated inside my head. My senses began to take in her energy—everything about her felt cat-like: inquisitive, adventurous, and a bit untamed.

As if granting me the grace to lose myself in thought, she shifted her focus toward the rope-and-wood bench swing that hung from The Gathering Place's big, old oak tree. With quick precision and athletic prowess, she embraced the art of swinging back and forth.

"I like to think of myself as the one who 'rescued' you. I've always been here, yet I'm also the one who has been silenced almost since the beginning."

The color of her eyes shone with depth and clarity, embodying mystery and intrigue. One moment, they appeared bluish, and the next, they looked greenish hazel. The marbling effect, mixed with the light, could make them change shades instantly. Yet, the intensity of her gaze remained constant—glittering like a shiny ornament.

"I remember you. But if I recall correctly, it was somewhat of a mixed bag with you always wanting to be in charge!"

My thoughts drifted to memories of my childhood as an explorer, a risk-taker who sometimes followed that part of me into dangerous and unsafe territory. I stood motionless, watching her pump her legs in unison as she swung higher and higher.

The one who looked so much like me but whom I'd mostly forgotten gave a glance over her shoulder and said, "I'm Athena!" Her voice slightly wavered as she swung with tremendous enthusiasm.

"The one who kept us moving forward by urging us to open doors and discover new things. Well—at least until our parents scared you so badly that you had to put us in the shadows with many of the others. But I understand. I mean, I get why you felt you had to do that. Your safety depended on it, for Pete's sake!"

I delved into my mind and instantly retrieved memory after memory, ignited by Athena's words. Had I always been aware of this? After being relinquished, placed in foster care, adopted, and then left to navigate an abusive, chaotic adoptive family, I had valid reasons to keep certain aspects of myself hidden. I allowed these personas—that could jeopardize my survival—to exist only behind the scenes. It felt true. As I reflected on the idea of enduring my childhood home, where my adoptive family needed me to be the person they demanded, my thoughts became increasingly clear on how I had to adapt to make it through. Then came the realization that these adaptations effectively severed me from my true developing self but ensured my safety during my youth. Or, let's just say—made me "safer."

But what were these modifications, or self-divisions, bringing me now as an adult? I began envisioning a recent photograph of myself smiling and looking so happy. Still, now I am picturing a more accurate image of myself, perhaps without an eye. Maybe even lacking a mouth, an arm, or feet to escape with. All of these are the adaptations I had to make to survive.

"Emma," Athena said, suddenly locking eyes with me. She had jumped from the swing, landing as gracefully as a cat.

"I am your creativity! I am your curiosity! Your fuel to keep exploring. I'm not just your belly when you take a breath; I'm also your backside that holds the tension while you slowly exhale. To breathe is to explore. To explore is to be alive. Creativity is the fuel that propels you forward. But Emma, I'm also the part of you our adoptive parents needed to eradicate. I'm the one they banned you from being. So, they convinced you—manipulated you—to kill me."

Athena was unlike any of the others I had invited to visit me at The Gathering Place: Tabitha—my delightful five-year-old; Mia—my younger, more self-doubting self; Lauren—the self who internalized my parents' sins; Baby Girl Lockridge—my infant self; and Kate—my confused but determined college self. These were parts of me, my vulnerable parts, that I knew well and felt could be consoled and offer wisdom. I hoped to update them with more accurate and helpful information I had learned from living a more reflective life in adulthood.

There was also one of my protector parts aptly named Justice, who is my 12-year-old self. Justice carried the world's weight and tried to correct all injustices. Like Athena, Justice was viewed as unacceptable by my parents and, consequently, by young me. In recent years, I have only begun to see them both as essential to my new way of being. They were, and are, integral to the most authentic parts of me.

Meeting with Athena felt somewhat like being plunged into an ice bath—exciting, hopeful, and a bit dangerous. Having her in the room while I was under the watchful eyes of my adoptive parents and family brought me shame, ridicule, and even physical harm. I was conditioned to keep my inquisitive part, Athena, tightly locked away.

Athena was the significant part of me who wondered why my mother had walked away, seemingly willingly, handing me over to strangers. I also pondered who my first family was, what they looked like, how they acted, and where they were. Most importantly, I longed to find them someday. She was also the part of me that yearned to explore a sense of awe and radical amazement.

Abraham J. Heschel, author of *Who Is Man?*, states, "Awe is more than an emotion; it's a way of understanding, an insight into something greater than ourselves. The beginning of awe is wonder, and the beginning of wisdom is awe. Curiosity nurtures knowledge; awe nurtures wisdom. The loss of awe leads to the avoidance of insight."

In my youth, I had to surrender my awe, curiosity, inquisitive nature, and authentic self. My parents suppressed much of my essence because they deemed me unacceptable.

There's a term called breadcrumbing. It's a form of manipulation that occurs when someone pretends to be interested in pursuing or developing a sincere relationship when, in reality, they have no interest. Since childhood, I learned to get by with less and less from my adoptive family, telling myself I should always be grateful that they took me in and raised me as their daughter. I believed them when they called me "special," even though their overall actions and behaviors did not reflect this to be true.

It saddens me to recall those occasional cold winter mornings when my dad would relent and say he'd take me to school instead of enduring the hour-and-a-half bus ride. I was overjoyed to spend this time alone with him. He was different when he wasn't under the watchful eye of my belittling mother. So, when he said he would "go out of his way" to take me, I felt special. Even though this meant he would take me at 6:30 a.m. and drop me in the empty schoolyard to wait until the school opened at 8:00 a.m., those mornings were incredibly cold. But I told myself I was special.

"I've missed you, Athena," I choked out, the lump in my throat growing.

The truth was, I had ached for her. Athena was one of the parts of me banished to linger, hidden in the shadows, so my adoptive family could remain comfortable and happy with their purchase of me. Athena gave me a warm smile that lit up my insides. I experienced a revelation, a sudden understanding that hit me all at once, making me wonder how I could have overlooked it.

"Let's take a walk, Emma."

I appreciated how she addressed me by name as if we were fellow travelers—equal in status. She represented more of my authentic self than I had permitted myself to be in decades. Only in hidden, stolen moments had I traversed a road less traveled. On this path, I became unafraid to be bold and courageous in speaking my truth rather than simply trying to keep the peace. As a peacekeeper and people-pleaser who created a shadow self to navigate my adoptive family, I had learned not to disrupt the connection, which I mistook for love, fearing it would lead to deprivation. This fear has been central to my experience as an adoptee. My shadow side, or my younger self, didn't realize that maintaining a connection at the cost of truth was a powerful way to lose oneself and endure a slow death of spirit. False peace is no peace: true, honest love is never an oppressive trauma bond.

The sun hung low in the cerulean sky, and the forceful wind from earlier had transformed into a cool breeze, carrying scents of rich earth, wild grasses, and sweet flowers. Like a magnet, I eagerly followed Athena down the lime-green grassy hill to the river, meandering through the enchanting, life-changing space I had come to cherish in my heart and affectionately refer to as The Gathering Place.

3

Green-Eyed Lady

"**B**reaker, breaker, good buddy! This is Spider Monkey," my 14-year-old brother Tim—two and a half years older than me—announced into the CB radio microphone. "What's your ten-twenty? Over."

The CB, or Citizens Band radio, is still widely used by semi-truck drivers for short-range communications, updates on road conditions, and general conversation on long cross-country drives. Unlike a walkie-talkie, only one person can transmit at a time on a single frequency channel.

"Ten-four, Spider Monkey, this is Big Trucker Bob! Just passing a convoy outside the 'Paris of the Plains,' Kansas City. Over."

My brother and I squealed with delight, having made our first contact with someone in CB radioland, using the CB base station radio Tim had just bought with the chore money he had saved. We excitedly began brainstorming our CB handle names when he set up the radio, antenna, and microphone on his room's dark brown hardwood desk.

"Ooh, I want mine to be 'Green-Eyed Lady!'"

Tim nodded in approval and told me he would be 'Spider Monkey,' after a character he'd recently seen in a comic book. I had chosen mine from a 1970s song by the band Sugarloaf. And I did have green eyes, after all. I'm unsure about the lady part since I was only twelve. However, the name made me feel older and wiser. It also made me feel like I was living the life of a secret agent.

Years later, I would discover that secret names were needed at other times. My birth mother went by a pseudonym during her stay at a maternity home for unwed mothers, and then much later, I created a whole new persona and name to author three books.

Tim looked at me in a panic, exclaiming, "What should I say now?!" We both burst into hearty laughter and quickly glanced at the CB radio language cheat sheet we had placed on his desk.

Tim and I rarely sat shoulder-to-shoulder, chair-to-chair in the same room, enjoying the same activity together. Feeling this connection was not lost on me. I had deeply missed my big brother since my younger days, looking up to him as my possible protector. At around five or six, my intense need to be close to him manifested in me sneaking into his bedroom at night, hoping to sleep there. I was also sure the workers I had watched build our house were still hiding in my closet—

now monsters. My brother represented a haven for me and a source of comfort that I longed for. It backfired, however, causing considerable upset for my parents and, in turn, getting us both into trouble.

Our parents would be furious when they discovered me in my brother's bed the following morning. Their screaming would jolt us both awake. Tim would look pale since he had no idea I had crept into his room in the middle of the night. As they yanked me out of my brother's room and down the hall by my five-year-old arm, all I felt was red-hot shame and guilt for getting him into trouble. And thinking, "What's wrong with me?"

Tim and I were adoptive siblings. We rarely discussed or shared our thoughts on our adoptions. He would only say, "My birth parents didn't want to know me, so why would I want to know them?"

However, he was aware from conversations he'd overheard between our parents and me that I *did* want to know where I came from. He'd also heard their scathing comments about how ungrateful and selfish I was for being curious.

Our relationship had always been strained by having adoptive parents who didn't foster or nurture a good connection between us. They seemed incapable of modeling healthy behavior overall. I always believed they did this to prevent Tim and me from forming any alliance that might weaken their control over us. The "divide and conquer" approach ensured that our parents consistently kept our sibling relationship from developing any healthy connection. They would, in turn, blame us for having a poor relationship.

Tim leaned into the mic, raising his eyebrows and touching his lips to the cold metal. "Ten-four, Big Trucker Bob! Have you seen any 'Smokey Bears?' Over." The exchange had Tim and me roaring with uncontrollable laughter, as we had just compared a policeman to a bear.

Big Trucker Bob responded immediately, saying, "Negatory, Spider Monkey. But I'm keepin' my eyes peeled for any 'Bears in the air' or 'Kojak with a Kodak.' Over."

"What does that mean?!" I quickly glanced at our cheat sheet and noticed he was still talking about highway patrol officers. Tim and I laughed at the idea of bears flying through the sky and having Kodak cameras on the ground.

"Emma, say something now," Tim urged. "Just say hello. But say it in CB lingo so he doesn't think you don't know what you're doing. OK?"

I instantly froze, not at all sure what to say. The last thing I wanted was to disappoint my brother, who seemed to be enjoying my company. It had been years since we had a good time together. I quickly looked over the cheat sheet again and leaned into the mic, careful not to put my lips on it as Tim did—because that would be gross.

"Breaker, breaker, Big Trucker Bob. My handle is 'Green-Eyed Lady.' Over." My racing heartbeat constricted my throat, making my words difficult to speak. But I'd done it! Looking at my brother beside me, I could see he was cheering me on. A huge smile lit up his heavily freckled face, and mine wore an even bigger one.

"Copy that, Green-Eyed Lady, that's a big ten-four! Come on," Big Trucker Bob replied.

Before I had a chance, the trucker came back over the CB radio, "Breaker, breaker, gotta stop to get some 'go juice.' Catch you on the flip-flop."

That was Big Trucker Bob's last transmission to us that night.

Looking back, Spider Monkey and Green-Eyed Lady's CB radio days were short-lived. Tim soon grew tired of the exchanges over the radio waves and became more interested in listening to acid-rock music with his headphones on. It became a one-person activity. When I'd ask to recreate those fun times with us laughing and coming up with CB lingo to say over the radio waves, Tim would reply, "Emma, the CB radio is for babies. Why don't you find a friend your age?"

This comment was a phrase he often repeated since he started first grade while I was still in kindergarten. I was heartbroken that he preferred to play with his newfound friends at his new school rather than with me. Once again, I retreated, surrendering to what seemed to be the true nature of our relationship—being isolated in our worlds that seldom intersected.

Decades later, I would attend my brother Tim's graveside service. He passed away at the age of 60 on a stretcher in the back of an ambulance on the way to the hospital after going into cardiac arrest. The heroic efforts of the paramedics to restart his heart had failed. Two years earlier, after his first heart attack, the doctor advised him to change his lifestyle or he would most certainly face an early death. Tim avoided confronting his chronic health issues, and his life was filled with substance abuse and self-sabotaging behaviors that went unaddressed.

He died in July 2020, before our parents did, and it fell to me to break the news to them. No one should have to tell their 88- and 92-year-old parents that their son has died. As long as I can remember, my dad would say, "You and your brother will have each other after your mother and I are gone."

However, things did not play out that way. I longed for my brother while he was alive, and now I yearn for him even more in his death.

4

Justice

The trickling stream meandering through the meadow at The Gathering Place overflowed its banks from the recent snowmelt. A dense thicket of fallen tree branches created vulnerable spots, overwhelming the stream and causing its waters to spread over the nearby land.

My gaze settled on a small, mint-colored frog with metallic green stripes perched on a rock near the water's edge. The sunlight highlighted his beauty, revealing his vibrant colors and hues. Having seen this frog many times, I named him "Fred." Fred and I seemed to share this place as our own. The meditative sound of water flowing over the various sizes of boulders in different colors helped me breathe and feel connected to everything around me. Sharing this moment with Fred deepened my desire for an open heart and mind.

The soft reeds that bent down to the ground provided a gentle cushion to sit on. The vibrant green that seemed to envelop me evoked feelings of liveliness, freshness, and creativity. In the stillness, my eyes caught movement within the lime-green growth surrounding the stream. At first, I thought the movement was just the valley breezes gently bending the grasses back and forth. But then I noticed movement with a different shape and color. My old friend, Justice, boldly stepped out from the dense greenery.

With her arm and hand waving, she shouted, "Hello!"

Jumping to my feet, I shouted, "Hello, Justice!"

"Hey, it's great to see you," Justice said, breathing heavily. "I've been searching for you near the tree and the swing. Then I decided to come down here by the stream."

I pressed down more grass beside me so she could sit. Justice looked happier than I'd seen her last time, which made me smile inside and out. Warm feelings surged within me—feelings of confidence that our conversations were renewing our spirit. Justice is both a part of me and a friend. She embodies the energetic side of me that approaches life optimistically, though she can sometimes be idealistic. She struggles with the idea that life isn't always fair, and when she can't accept her reality, it causes her pain. However, even while enduring the pain that often comes with fighting for a specific cause, Justice is one of my most resilient and tenacious parts, and she has served me well over the years.

I marvel at Justice's ability to stand and fight and how she can truly sink her teeth into advocating for us. I think of Justice as my loving self who wants nothing more than to be my cheerleader. She was determined to find my birth story and birth parents because she knew it was what we needed. She also retrieved my adoption files, which had been legally prohibited to me. Justice felt utterly justified in breaking into the adoption agency to get our information. She also stood up to my adoptive mother when I was 17 and threatened to strike her back if she ever tried to hit me again. In more recent years, Justice was instrumental in reclaiming my life and ending my decades-long use of alcohol as a coping mechanism. And it was Justice who stood strong and made valiant efforts to help me escape a sociopathic, exploitative therapist whose intent was to consume me.

I cherish her. Yet, she was a part of me that my younger parts felt needed to be silenced. Justice was too dangerous for their safety and well-being. To survive authoritative, narcissistic, and abusive parents, I had to develop many strategies to stay protected. I learned to temper Justice's spiritedness and only express her when it was safe.

But Justice was—and is—strong. She's resilient. Tenacious. My adult self is incredibly welcoming and grateful for Justice. Like with Athena, my curious and creative self, I plan to help my other parts (especially the younger ones) recognize the beauty and promise these two bring. Because of my intense integrative work, I can now update my system and sound the all-clear alarm. Freedom from the hypervigilance and bondage to the inauthentic identity I was forced to develop in my youth is now mine. It's a choice that's now solely mine to make.

"You seem happy! Everything going OK?" I said as

I playfully punched her on the arm.

"Yeah, pretty darn great. I feel so much better these days, and that's part of why I'm here." Justice shifted around, flattening more grass as she turned to look me in the eye. "I wanted to thank you for coming to talk with the others and to let you know what a huge difference it's made. It's like you allowed them to talk to each other and not feel so alone anymore. And you know what? I think they're starting to feel seen and heard. It's all thanks to you coming back and listening to them. It's what they, and the rest of us, have always wanted! So, thanks!"

Justice concluded by hitting me on the arm.

"Wow." That was all I could say. I started to play with the tall grass around me as I let Justice's words sink in.

She continued, "I think it's cool that you've started remembering Athena and me. You know, allowing us to come back into your life. And I don't just mean sometimes—like before. I feel like I'm back as a part of you most of the time now. I feel like we can fully breathe again."

With a huge smile, I pulled back my left sleeve to reveal my new tattoo.

"No way! How pretty! What does it mean?" Justice asked.

"It's the Sanskrit symbol for the word 'breathe,'" I said.

Justice and I sat in the tall grass by the stream at The Gathering Place, nodding knowingly. An iridescent dragonfly hovered nearby, its transparent wings reflecting the sun's rays. The next moment, it skimmed away, darting forward, backward, and all around.

"You know, breathing is like flying," I said. "You need that expansive inhale—matched by an equally expansive exhale to lift off the ground. It's a form of letting go. You must fully breathe to fly and to experience awe. I believe that when you don't, you let fear become a vice that shuts you off from everything. And then you drop like a lead weight."

After a long silence, I asked, "You know, it's been almost a year since Dad died and a year and a half since Mom. How are you?"

"Yeah, I've been thinking about that. Grief is a strange creature. It's hard to know when it will strike, how it will manifest, or if it will come at all. And if it has already occurred, will it return?" Justice's eyebrows knitted together, and she suddenly seemed smaller than she had moments earlier. "Do you know what the hardest part for me was?"

I waited and listened.

"We fulfilled Mom and Dad's wishes to die in their home. Yet they were still so freakin' miserable. They still somehow held us responsible for even their old age. Responsible for not being able to save them from death. *As if!*"

I nodded, took a deep breath, and said, "They showed me something in their death, though … I learned how I *do not* want to die. Leaving this life without love and integrity is not what I'm striving for. It's not what I want for any of us. I want to choose to look at death as the ultimate invitation. Something we're all going to get the opportunity to do. Just as was our birth. Instead of dragging everyone down a deep, dark hole with me, I hope to be loving, grateful, and courageous. I'll learn everything I can until the very end. At least during my time on this Earth."

"Yes. That sounds right. It feels like it fits. Choosing to breathe for however long we're here," Justice said with a nod. "Do you think the others agree? Is Tabitha coming around? Of course, I *know* Athena agrees!" We both chuckled at the thought of Athena, our ever-curious one, not getting it. We both knew she was miles ahead of us.

My body stilled. I gently placed my hand on my chest, feeling the heat of my skin. "No, some of the others don't agree yet. Most don't even know they're free now. It will take more time to convince them they're safe."

Justice crawled over to get a better look at our friend Fred, the mint-green speckled frog still perched on the rock near the gently flowing waters of the stream. She drew nearer, asking him a rhetorical question, "What do you think we should do, little Freddy?! How can we convince the others we're free now and can all hop to The Gathering Place whenever we want?!"

I leaned in. "I really like how you phrased that because we both know that if we try to strong-arm them into going—and if they think they'll never be able to return to what's familiar—we'll lose them. How did you get so wise, Justice?!"

"Pretty awesome, right?!" Justice said with a broad grin.

5

Snicklefritz

Not long ago, I stood in a hotel room, gazing out the window at Golden, Colorado's lightly snow-frosted foothills. My view included the Golden High School football field and the ongoing Thursday night game. This was the exact field where my adoptive father had played high school football in the early 1950s. I tried to imagine him running up and down the green field, brightly lit by stadium lights, accompanied by the sounds of a marching band and the piercing blasts of the referees' whistles.

My often gregarious adoptive father stood 6'2" and had a booming, commanding voice. He was generally well-liked and could be immensely entertaining with his charismatic personality and charm. When he walked into a room, everyone felt it. He hailed from this small town of Golden, Colorado, nestled in the foothills just west of Denver. In my dad's youth, Golden was the remnant of the earlier mining days, but now it has been transformed into an outdoor wonderland and popular tourist destination for summer hiking, mountain biking, river rafting, and fishing. It's a convenient stop for winter visitors heading to the Rocky Mountain ski resorts, only two hours away. Golden is also home to the premier research university focused on science and engineering, the Colorado School of Mines. And yes, it's the home of the renowned Coors Brewery, founded in 1873.

My adoptive father, Arthur Stevens, was an entrepreneur, busy building his empire, as he and my mother referred to his successful business and career. However, his success came at a price, dividing his time and attention to the point where he neglected his role as husband and father. He was frequently absent and inaccessible to his two adoptive children.

After discovering they were infertile soon after they married, my parents decided to create their family through infant adoption, which was not uncommon in the 1960s, now referred to as the "Baby Scoop Era." During this period, from the late 1940s through the early 1970s, many unmarried pregnant women were coerced—by family, religious institutions, and social workers—into placing their babies for adoption. First, my parents adopted Tim, and then two and a half years later, they adopted me from a different biological family.

I saw my father strike my brother to the ground in submission countless times. Tim did not reflect my father and his idea of what a "man" should be. Both my parents believed they could beat us and mold us into being acceptable to them. When their efforts didn't succeed, they would double down. So, I'm not entirely sure Tim would agree that good times with my dad outweighed those with my mom.

My fond memories of being with my dad come from family trips to the ocean and playing in the waves. He let me climb onto his shoulders while the waves crashed around us. Tim and I took turns seeing who could stay up the longest. The slippery suntan oil on my dad's dark, tanned skin made staying perched on his shoulders precarious. Then, a thundering wave would crash in, sweeping my brother and me into the saltwater and making us howl with laughter.

Later, when I was 22, I joined my parents on a trip to Destin, Florida, where they had rented a beach house. We went in October, which made this particular trip unforgettable. I had never been to a beach in the off-season.

My dad and I were crabbing—just my dad and me—walking the beach and enjoying the tranquility of the shore. Each of us had our crab-catching nets, and we only needed to wade waist-deep into the clear blue water over a soft, sugar-white ocean bottom to see the crabs. The visibility was remarkable. The beauty was matched only by the sky, robin's-egg blue and dotted with pastel-colored, cotton-like clouds.

"Dad, look to your left! Do you see it?!" The large brown crab with orange claws was initially motionless, but it almost danced once we saw it. The ocean waves moved us back and forth, causing me to panic, thinking my bare foot was sure to feel the crunch of a crab claw at any moment!

My dad stealthily scooped up the sideways-walking

crab in his net and kept walking. I was impressed by his steadiness in capturing the crab as it darted back and forth across the sands of the ocean floor—right next to his bare legs and toes. These crabs were to be our dinner that night. I didn't know who would cook them, but I wasn't concerned.

I spotted and scooped up the next crab and then the next. Each time I found one, my heart raced. But what thrilled me most was spending this rare time with my father, laughing and creating memories with him.

I joined my parents on this trip because I had recently quit—honestly, I had crashed and burned at my first advertising job in Dallas, Texas. I had taken my freshly-minted degree in journalism off to this new opportunity right after graduation, not realizing that I carried my unresolved past of adoption trauma and family coercive control with me. At that time, I lacked the understanding or language to reflect on my feelings, let alone do anything about it. I lasted only three months.

"How are things going, Snicklefritz?" That was one of his nicknames for me. I always felt a warmth when he used that term of endearment. It also meant I wasn't in trouble or facing any danger—physically or emotionally. While the physical abuse had stopped by my late teens, the manipulation and coercive control tactics continued.

However, this moment halted me in time, and I knew it was special. It felt significant, much more so than all the other moments that come and go, big and small, stringing together to make up the totality of our lives.

I don't remember what led to his question on that

bright October day as we walked through the crystal-clear waters of that Florida beach, but I recall feeling this was the question I'd always wished he had asked me when I was four, then seven, ten, and through my teens and into adulthood. Things like: "How do you feel about growing up?" "How do you feel about being adopted?" "Do you miss your birth mom? What about your birth dad?"

Or how about this: "I'm sorry your mother treats you so poorly, both mentally and physically. And I'm sorry for beating you with a belt or other times hitting you with my bare hands. I'm sorry I've let your mother beat you and your brother throughout your childhood."

And the ultimate, *"I'm sorry I didn't protect you."*

At 22, I wouldn't have had the language or awareness to express the emotions that had continuously resided in my gut, even if he had asked me what I wished he had. I didn't fully understand my life revelations until I was in my late 40s and early 50s. Much more searching, bumping into walls, researching, and discovering had to happen before I began to see my life more clearly.

Next, something far more pressing occurred. My drifting thoughts suddenly returned to the present moment.

"Dad ... why are those people on the beach waving their arms and shouting at us?" A rush of adrenaline coursed through me.

"What?" I mumbled to myself, unable to hear my fellow beachgoers from the edge of the shoreline. I watched intently as their arms flapped like birds attempting to take flight, and then I saw them with outstretched arms and fingers pointing. I saw their concern in that direction, just over my left shoulder.

"*Shark*, Dad, *shark!*"

The sudden panic sent my dad and me scrambling through water that felt as constricting and heavy as quicksand. Moments stretched like hours as we tried to move from waist-deep water to knee-deep water, finally finding our footing to sprint to shore. We doubled over, our lungs burning for air once we reached safety. Looking at each other, we noticed our crabs still precariously caught in our nets. Turning to face the ocean, we searched for the shark that had terrorized us, making us think he would have us for a snack. We saw his fin as he lingered for a while before gliding silently back into deeper waters.

The locals on the beach explained that sharks come closer to the shoreline to feed during the fall months. They target distracted sea turtles as their dinner since they also feed in shallow, soft-bottomed habitats.

This near-shark attack is one of my favorite memories of my dad and me. Not only was it a thrilling shared experience, but it was also something I'll always hold close to me when thinking of him. I recall how we worked together to survive a precarious situation. I remember being 22 years old, feeling like I was failing miserably in the city where I had been working, unsure of how to help myself. I struggled with the emotional confusion of being adopted while growing up in a chaotic, abusive home. There was so much angst I hadn't reconciled yet. Regretfully, it had nearly turned into a genuine conversation between my dad and me, with whom I had shared much of my life.

6

The Good, Faithful Adopted Soldier

At The Gathering Place, anything is possible. The skies can be bright, blue, clear, or sometimes filled with dense granite-grey clouds connecting and functioning as a single ecosystem. This is another example of how everything is interconnected. Even clouds collaborate as one.

I have known how to breathe since I first entered this world, as we all do. However, The Gathering Place has been my teacher, showing me how to desire to inhale and exhale more intentionally, deeply, and fully. Through its wonder and awe, it has provided a safe space that has taught me how to choose to breathe with greater intentionality. This type of breathing, as opposed to shallow chest breathing, soothes my hypervigilance and clears the way to unearth my long-exiled parts that, of late, have become fully able to experience the state of being in awe.

I've learned to recognize my identity by gathering and accepting moments of awe—sometimes just seconds of magical, often heartbreakingly beautiful, experiences. Those times have soothed my wounds and calmed my most profound doubts and fears, allowing my soul to reclaim its true essence. I believe everything belongs and is connected, and I am a part of it all, just as we all are. I recognize my craving for moments of awe. These moments have fundamentally changed me and taught me to maintain an open heart so I won't miss the next life-changing opportunity. When I choose to breathe, I seek and am present for the gravitational pull of wonderment. I do this without resisting the incredible, underlying mystery that exists everywhere, all the time, which is the ultimate invitation.

My adoptive brother Tim did not choose to embrace life fully. I know he experienced moments of awe and wonder. He loved his five children, four of whom were quadruplets; they were his passion. However, Tim didn't love himself enough to learn how to bring health into his life. Instead, much of his life was plagued by substance abuse, failed relationships, and unrealized potential.

I yearn for one last conversation with him—a reconciliation, a chance to repair old wounds that remained unattended because our parents made sure we didn't compare notes about our abusive childhood, which might have made them accountable. My older brother, Tim, did not choose to breathe in a life-giving way and died shortly after turning 60. I don't blame him for this, but I deeply regret that he didn't consider doing this for himself and for those who loved him.

I've built a new addition to The Gathering Place. It symbolizes the final resting places of my mom, dad, and brother. This section features majestic pink flowering crabapple trees and vast snow-capped views of the Rocky Mountains in the distance. It serves as a time and space where I can share all my thoughts with them without fear of repercussions. The Gestalt therapeutic approach, called "The Empty Chair" technique, can be hugely therapeutic. The idea is that even though a person is not present, you direct your words and gestures to an empty chair and imagine that person sitting in it while you talk. This method of therapy can be engaging and transformational, allowing you to respond to unresolved feelings from a new perspective.

"The weather is wonderful today," I addressed my mom, dad, and brother. "I have a few things to share. Now that I've made space for you here at my Gathering Place, I'm confident you'll hear me."

I paused to watch a squirrel scamper up the side of a crabapple tree, then out onto a limb extending over my family's grave sites. As I observed, writer and spiritual teacher Richard Rohr's words came to mind: "Nature is the one song of praise that never stops singing."

I continued, "I am a survivor, Mom and Dad. I survived being relinquished and adopted at birth, and I endured the many ways you vehemently tried to ignore that I came to you with a history you were not part of. I endured all the ways you sought to extinguish who I truly was, creating a shadow self that fawned to please you and be who you needed me to be."

I rested against the tall crabapple tree, feeling its rough bark against the small of my back and taking a few deep breaths.

"I survived through all the ways you never took responsibility for your actions and how you gaslit me into believing that it was my responsibility to bear and be accountable for it. I survived being told by you that my birth family, whom you didn't even know, were considered inferior and were cut from a 'lesser' cloth."

"Now, wait just a minute, you ungrateful, silly girl! You felt so put upon, huh? We gave you everything! You wouldn't have survived without us!" I hear the harsh, accusatory voice of the mother who raised me.

"You know what, Mom? Here at The Gathering Place—*my Gathering Place*—we treat each other respectfully, even if we disagree with what others say," I said.

My mother's familiar, angry, disapproving tone suddenly reminded me of something my mother's sister had said recently. "You know, your mom could be a real guerrilla." I didn't even have to ask her what she meant. I knew.

I ignored my mother's attack and said, "I survived. You never asked me what it felt like to be an adopted person. You never heard me when I asked questions about my birth family. You never tried or wanted to see 'me.' You never permitted me to grieve the loss of my first family or acknowledge my depression. You never seemed to understand that you were genetic strangers to me. We didn't mirror one another in any way. So, every time you said, 'We don't even remember you were adopted,' you erased a part of me."

I heard my father's booming voice: *"You can't talk to your mother like that! She sacrifices everything for you and your brother. Tell your mother you love her and straighten out this lousy attitude of yours!"*

"Mom ... Dad ... this is *my* Gathering Place. It's *my* time to express everything I could never communicate because I didn't have the language or feel safe. My trauma vocabulary developed much later after significant work on my self-development in uncovering my true self. You never helped nurture that in me. You never taught me how to self-regulate my emotions—the way parents are supposed to for their children. It was quite the opposite. Because of your feelings of inadequacy and narcissistic tendencies to be authoritarian and totalistic in your parenting style, you deliberately and intentionally stifled me."

I sat down on the still-damp earth, placing my hands over my face. My palms absorbed the heat radiating from my cheeks. With my knees tucked into my chest, I noticed how my feet felt firmly planted on the ground. At first, my breathing was shallow, but then I began to take long, slow breaths, holding at the top and releasing the air slowly through my nose. Before long, my racing heart slowed, and my parasympathetic system returned online, making me feel clearer and sharper, and overall, a sense of well-being returned.

In Viktor Frankl's book, *Man's Search for Meaning*, he states, "Between stimulus and response, there is a space. In that space is our power to choose our response. In our response lies our growth and freedom."

I know this to be true: *life is better, but I must fight for it daily.* What do I think a happy life looks like? It involves living from a deep center, being contemplative, practicing love that refuses to settle for false peace, being authentic, and being inclusive of everyone—even those different from myself. I can't manufacture my transformation, but I can stay attentive and be ready for when the shift comes that brings growth.

"Mom and Dad, I'm saddened you didn't do your interior work. We are all called to engage in this journey during our lifetimes, not just for our own peace but also for the sake of those we love. I feel sorrow when I think about how to love you; I had to form a traumatic bond with you, which is not love at all."

Writer and spiritual leader Rob Bell articulates my definition of love, one that aligns with consensus reality: "Love demands freedom. It always has, and it always will."

"Your love hurt me and destroyed my brother Tim. No one should ever make someone their whipping post to vent their self-hatred. The methods you used have all been identified by mind control expert Dr. Steven Hassan as a cult-like tactics he called the BITE model. BITE is an acronym standing for four authoritarian ways to maintain control over people by undue influence: behavior, information, thought, and emotional control and manipulation. You may ask, how do I know this? To survive the psychological nightmare you both subjected me to, I had to learn about techniques such as these."

My body was shaking again. Anger had come to visit. I consoled myself and all my parts, who were more than a little nervous about me speaking the truth so loudly. I comforted them and assured them I was expressing long-overdue, healthy feelings.

My mother's shrill voice pierced the air as she exclaimed, *"After all we've done for you! We just knew you would be the kind of child who would have trouble being adopted. It was written all over your face when you cried after we told you at three years old. How could you be so ungrateful?"*

My mother spat her words, followed by my father, who added, *"How do you think it made your mother feel when you cried for a woman who threw you away? Your mother gave up everything for you and your brother. You were the light of her life!"*

My dad's primary concern was for my mother's feelings first. But I was the child. His words completely discounted my feelings. Their harsh words were meant not only to convey that I should be ashamed but also that I *am* shame.

I responded calmly and quietly, "I was three years old and gave you an honest reaction to a sad story you had just told me. How could you shame a child so young? Being adopted is *not my fault!* I had no control over the situation. But it seems like you always needed someone to blame for the fact that I wasn't your biological child and that I came to you with a history. I didn't mirror you in any way. You needed to project all your unresolved infertility issues onto Tim and me to try to make yourselves feel better. Do you realize how emotionally immature that was? Hitting your children into submission and manipulating them into becoming parentified children is cruel!"

I researched that parentification describes the reversal of the roles of parent and child, in which a child's natural development is disrupted. This role reversal, first identified and named by psychiatrist Ivan Boszormenyi-Nagy, can create far-reaching adverse effects on the child's mental and physical health.

I closed my eyes and gently rubbed my forehead. Although my parents weren't supposed to be talking, I could still hear their voices!

I suddenly realized they weren't responding to what I was saying *at all*; their voices came from a part of me that had taken over for them. It was likely a part of me that observed my parents so I could shape myself to be more pleasing to them and better avoid harm.

Like most of us, I had unwittingly incorporated my critical parent, or superego, as world-renowned Austrian neurologist and founder of psychoanalysis Sigmund Freud taught. Freud once said, "The ideals contributing to the formation of the superego include not just the morals and values we learn from our parents, but also the ideas of right and wrong we acquire from society and our culture." And more recently, writer and spiritual coach Neal Allen refers to the superego as "the snarky little bully in your head" in his 2023 book *Better Days: Claim Your Inner Critic.*

Once I became aware that I was conversing with my inner critic and not my parents, I softened and embraced this part of myself that had shown up in the newly created area of The Gathering Place, where my parents' and brother's grave markers are located. I then responded with love by extending grace. That's when a young girl suddenly appeared before me.

"What's your name, little one? I'm grateful you've come to visit me." I had been conversing with her, not my parents.

"Mallory," said the girl, who looked about four. She wore a plaid pleated skirt and a plain, long-sleeved white shirt like a school uniform. It appeared at least two sizes too large.

"You shouldn't talk that way about my mommy and daddy. They've given me everything. I'd be in the gutter if they hadn't saved me from a mom who threw me away! You'll get me into twouble if you keep saying those kinda things."

Mallory, whose name means "unlucky," had flushed red cheeks, and her tiny shoulders were pulled up almost to her ears. Here she was, standing her ground, defending our adoptive parents, who were the only ones she ever consciously remembered knowing.

"Mallory, I'm so happy you're here in this new section of our Gathering Place! The others and I have been looking forward to meeting you and having the chance to talk," I said, focusing all my attention on her.

Mallory scrunched her shoulders a bit higher and asked, "Why?"

Excited, I responded, "Well, to give you a turn at the rope-and-wood bench swing, of course!"

"I can't! My parents would be mad if they knew I was playing with you. I only came here, to this place, whatever you call it, to tell you to *'cut it out.'* That's what my mommy and daddy said I was to tell you. *'Tell her to stop talking like a widiculous, ungrateful, selfish fool!'*"

"Wow," I said, "that's a heavy load for you to carry, Mallory. How old are you?"

"I'm four."

"How old do you think ou … your parents are?" I stopped short of telling her they were *our* parents.

"I dunno. Pwetty old, I guess."

"That's right, Mallory! They are much older than you, which makes them adults. They should let you be a kid—it's *not* your job to take care of them. How does that make you feel?"

Mallory slowly blinked and said, "Hard. I never seem to do it right. The way they want me to."

Although I was grateful for this conversation and that Mallory trusted me enough to discuss things with her, my heart broke when I realized the cost of the burden our parents had placed on her.

"Yes, I know. I understand how hard you tried to please, defend, and accept them as your parents. In doing so, you had to believe everything they told you without question. I'm so proud of you and how diligently you've worked to keep the peace all these years! You helped us survive."

"They tell me what to think. I get into twouble when I don't mind them. Is wanting to play sometimes so bad?" Mallory's question did not seem rhetorical; she genuinely sought an answer.

I stood and offered her my hand. She slowly placed her warm, tiny hand in mine. I smiled and looked into her face, noticing her watery, owl-like green eyes. "Are you ready for your turn on the swing at The Gathering Place?"

Mallory quickly nodded and said, "I guess a few minutes would be OK!"

7

Permission to Breathe

"Emma, this time, I'd like you to pause and take a long, slow, deep, full inhale. At the top, give yourself space to take a final sip, hold it for five more seconds, and then slowly exhale for a full five seconds. Then repeat."

Laura, my yoga therapist, was teaching me mindful meditation and body awareness. We sat on our yoga mats facing one another as I attempted to enter a state of relaxation that would enable me to focus solely on the tone and timbre of her melodic voice.

I guessed that Laura had noticed, after asking me to breathe mindfully, that my shoulders instantly raised to my ears while my lungs filled in a mere two seconds. Instead of relaxing and breathing slowly for a count of five, I ended up in a mild panic, holding my breath for an inordinate amount of time. My exhales were more like urgent blasts, similar to the release of a suddenly untied inflated balloon.

Laura is working towards earning her yoga therapy certification. Yoga therapists use an integrative mind-body practice that extends beyond a yoga studio. This practice demands a passion for yoga and the desire to support others on their journey to physical, mental, and emotional well-being. Laura needed willing participants to assist her in obtaining in-person training hours so she could work with clients one-on-one, applying yoga techniques to specific health conditions.

I'd been fortunate enough to participate regularly in Laura's well-attended studio yoga classes and was eager to help. We had a good rapport, so I knew I would be in safe and capable hands while assisting her in achieving her required yoga therapist hours. My experiences with Laura proved invaluable in unlocking some key core issues, namely hypervigilance, that have been challenging me for most of my life.

After I attempted regulated, mindful breathing, I let out a nervous belly laugh. A bit embarrassed, I realized that laughing at my performance was a distraction. It was my way of sidestepping something, albeit unconsciously; however, I knew deep down that it needed to be addressed if I genuinely wanted to be on a path of restoration.

"Emma, tell me about the tattoo on your arm. What does it mean to you?" Laura's intense eye contact was kind yet imploring.

My gaze immediately shifted to the soft area of my left inner forearm, where I had a fresh tattoo. Touching it, I began explaining to Laura that it was the Sanskrit symbol for the word "breathe." I noticed how frequently

I hold my breath, not only during tense moments but also as a general habit. I hoped that the symbol on my arm would act as a prompt rather than merely a cool decorative image I wore on my body.

Staring intently at my tattoo, I felt the irony of having a reminder on my arm to breathe. My adult daughter had accompanied me when I had this symbol permanently inscribed just a few months prior. The symbol resonated deeply with my experience as a relinquished-at-birth adoptee, where I've often felt the need to make myself small to avoid taking up too much space.

Breathing seemed to take too long and made me expand. What would happen if I did? In my psyche, it felt like rejection and abandonment. Abandonment resulted in deprivation—both emotionally and physically. Thus, taking the time to breathe deeply was a risk I wasn't willing to take. Unconsciously, my memory of being relinquished by my mother at birth ruptured my nervous system. I can only imagine how my infant self felt when the symbiotic bond of mother and child was abruptly severed, never to reunite. I must have longed for her, my lost infant self, especially during my first experience in the world. It's a fissure I've never adequately grieved or fully acknowledged.

As a result, hypervigilance took residence in my body. I didn't know its name, but I felt its presence. It has been renting space within me for a very long time and honed by being adopted into a family without emotional sobriety or maturity. I had been relinquished and adopted into a family of strangers, strangers who had not acknowledged their grief or psyches before bringing two babies into their home. Much to their dismay, neither of us mirrored their interests, personality, or appearance. Our differences angered our parents and even influenced how our grandparents and other family members treated us. They treated us like the strangers we were: two children from an unknown place.

Our parents unleashed their anger and frustration on both my brother and me. I developed an even stronger muscle of hypervigilance and adaptability in response to their unpredictable behavior. These became my tools for survival. And what a muscle I built! My seemingly innate ability to be tenacious and resilient served me well when I needed to tuck, duck, and roll—both physically and mentally—from my parents' everyday abusive behaviors.

My brother Tim's temperament did not serve him as well. While we both endured trauma from relinquishment, adoption, and an exceptionally dysfunctional home, I seemed to process things differently than Tim. People-pleasing and perfectionism were my adapted ways to stay further out of harm's way. Tim, in turn, did not conform; he only withered—his spirit crushed at an early age.

"Emma?" Laura's soft, encouraging voice pulled me back into the room. "Emma, what if you permitted yourself to breathe? I mean, truly breathe?"

Laura's tenderness brought tears to my eyes, and a flood followed. It was as if Jupiter, the planet of wisdom and good fortune, had aligned with my consciousness, clearly showing me how my reluctance to take long, slow, deep breaths was inextricably linked to my fears of abandonment and feelings of unworthiness. What if I took too much time to breathe? Everyone might leave the room. This realization was painful yet revelatory, allowing me to examine this long-held core belief and understand that it was false. I've acted my entire life as if it were true, but I've reached a moment where I can either continue believing it or change it to reflect the present. And the present tells me I'm human and deserve to breathe the air around me fully.

What if I choose to breathe?

I threw my arms around Laura as my words tumbled out, trying to help her understand what had happened. It felt like she had given me the key to a new dimension. She looked concerned yet relieved when I explained how my tears were as much from joy as from sorrow. Making these connections, linking my past to my present, fueled my journey and desire to become more fully me.

Fear leads to hypervigilance. Hypervigilance stifles curiosity. A lack of curiosity hinders creativity. The decline of creativity erases freedom. These words by Richard Rohr came to me.

Suddenly, I felt ready to try again. I softened my body, relaxed my facial muscles, and slid my shoulder blades down my back. Next, I closed my eyes and began honoring myself by taking a long, slow, deep breath into my lungs for five seconds, taking one last sip of air, holding it at the top for five seconds, slowly exhaling for five seconds, and pushing one last time at the bottom to expel any remaining breath. Then I repeated.

After completing many mindful breathing rounds, Laura stayed in the room the whole time and was still there for me. When we said our goodbyes that day, I thanked her and hoped she understood what a priceless gift she had given me.

Months later, Laura and I met in Denver at Snooze, a charming little breakfast spot. We shared coffee and pineapple pancakes while catching up. I had sent her this chapter of my manuscript, which relates directly to the title of this book.

Laura leaned in and said, "Emma, when I read what you wrote about your experience with breathwork combined with the bodywork we did, it made me *so happy*! It's why I've chosen to immerse myself in a profession that celebrates and promotes combining mind, body, and spirit for well-being. Your connections during our sessions led you to integrate a valuable discovery! I was elated to be your guide."

We sat at the two-top table next to a large picture window, and I gazed at the captivating pink flowering crabapple trees and the vibrant new lime-green growth from warmer temperatures. The rich scent of earth filled the air. It felt as though I was "double-dipping" in the chance to enjoy one of my favorite seasons since spring began over a month ago in my city of Tulsa, Oklahoma. It is wonderful to be with someone who truly "gets it." The energy of the reciprocity is ineffable. I couldn't help but feel a warm sense of home while connecting with my friend, Laura, and remembering to embrace nature's healing essence. With wholehearted intention, I am choosing to breathe.

8

Talks with Tim

"**Y**ou know, Mom and Dad don't believe you stole your adoption records. They think you made that up to protect the adoption agency. They believe the social worker gave them to you," my brother Tim told me when we both went to our grandmother's funeral in Golden, Colorado in 2006. Tim and his family now lived in Seattle, and my husband, my children, and I lived in Laguna Beach, California. Tim and I didn't get the chance to talk often.

"Well, believe it because I did it!" Although I was grateful for not getting caught, I still wanted recognition for what I viewed as a heroic effort in both obtaining my records and tackling the daunting challenge of actually finding my birth mother. It stirred resentment in me that I had always felt underestimated.

"How'd you do it? How did you even know where to look for the files?" Tim asked.

"It was crazy. I really didn't know. I had been in a

meeting at the adoption agency, speaking with the social worker, but I hadn't looked around much. I didn't even realize she had a letter with my birth mom's real name on it until that meeting. She gave me a copy of the letter but blacked out the signature. I couldn't believe my birth mother had written the letter! The agency would never have known her true identity if she hadn't. That means I wouldn't have had much chance to find out either."

I continued, focused on recalling how I had stolen my adoption records. "After that initial meeting with the adoption agency in Denver, I drove back to Tulsa, consumed by thoughts of how to get the letter. At that time, Colorado's adoption records were sealed, even for adult adoptees. I also knew that my birth mom likely signed my birth certificate using a fictitious name. By the end of the ten-hour drive home, I was determined to break in and obtain the letter and the rest of my adoption files. I developed a simple plan to go under the cover of darkness, taking precautions by dressing in black and using gloves, a hat, and a flathead screwdriver." I paused, looking for Tim's reaction.

"And you did all of this by yourself?" Tim asked, his eyebrows raised and knitted together.

"No, my boyfriend helped me. We went together and broke into the adoption agency. It was dark, and no one was around. My boyfriend didn't have to try very hard with the lock on the front door before we had it open. From there, I instinctively walked to the only closed door I saw and opened it. It was a large closet with file cabinets and four or five labeled boxes on the floor. First, I opened the unlocked file cabinet closest to me and found file after file of adoption records marked by year and name. They all appeared to be more recent files. I shifted my focus to the marked file boxes on the floor. I remember pausing, feeling both scared and excited at the same time. The thought of possibly being arrested at any moment nearly paralyzed me, but I continued moving forward. I discovered many adoptee records organized alphabetically on microfiche tapes when I opened the first box labeled 1960-1965."

As I recounted my story to Tim, I was transported back to the adoption agency's closet with my flashlight, thinking *I might have just found my records! They must be somewhere in this film since the years correspond to the year I was born and adopted.*

But I still didn't know. I had to view the tapes to be sure.

"And then I urged my boyfriend, 'We have to go to a library. They're open until 9:00 PM. I need to use their microfiche viewer to find my information among all these reels! We've got to take this entire box and go! Right now!'"

Tim's eyes were wide, and his hands rubbed the tops of his legs, looking anxious.

"I used the library's microfiche viewer to examine reel after reel from the stolen box, which contained all the documented adoptions for the agency from 1960 to 1965. There were hundreds!"

While sharing the story of my heist with my brother, I realized that the last time we were this engaged in conversation was during our CB radio days. That was decades ago when he was Spider Monkey and I was the Green-Eyed Lady.

"As the library's closing time approached, I became concerned that I wouldn't locate my file in time. I tried to move faster. I panicked when the librarian came over and told me I had 15 minutes to finish. That's when I discovered your information, Tim! I copied everything and continued scrolling until I eventually found mine! I barely finished copying before being politely escorted out of the building." My heart was pounding as I remembered that surreal night of stealing my *own* birth records.

"It wasn't until I was back in the car that I realized I had to return the stolen box. I couldn't keep all those hundreds of adoptee files! So, my boyfriend and I agreed to return to the agency, break in again, and put the box back in the closet where I had found it."

My memories of that night remain vivid. I recalled how certain I was that I saw flashing police lights and heard sirens, with police running on foot to handcuff me. When they didn't come that night, I remained convinced they would eventually arrive. I thought it was only a matter of time.

But they never did.

I looked at Tim and said, "When I had the box of files and found your information right before I found my own, I couldn't resist getting it for you! I've been holding onto them since I stole mine in 1987. That was 19 years ago! I haven't told you because I was uncertain how you'd feel about it." I was anxious for his response.

"I don't want it."

"Really?" I waited. "Why not?"

For most of my life, Tim was the only other adopted person I knew, and we rarely discussed it. I don't think we had the language to have a meaningful conversation. Tim didn't seem interested in learning about his biological family.

"Well, OK. I'll keep holding onto them in case you ever change your mind. Maybe one of your five children will be curious one day."

That day never came. Tim died 14 years later and is now buried right beside our grandparents and parents in the Golden, Colorado Cemetery, with the Rocky Mountains as the backdrop. That was one of the last conversations I had with my brother.

~

The Gathering Place allows me to revisit relationships where I want to bring understanding, comfort, and repair. I asked my brother, Tim, to meet me under the big, old oak tree. I wanted to have a conversation with him that I never had while he was alive. This is part of the magic of this place.

Our parents undermined our relationship since I joined the family as his little sister. Tim and I came together by forces beyond our control and were instructed to act as siblings. But we didn't know each other. We didn't even know our parents. Nonetheless, we all lived under one roof, pretending to be a family that knew each other. I tried desperately to follow my parents' script, but I never understood it or got it right. My life seemed like a Rubik's Cube puzzle—for me, it was unsolvable.

"Hey, Tim." I walked over and sat beside him in the shade of the tree. He looked surprised to find himself at The Gathering Place.

"Hey, how did I get here?" Tim asked, glancing around.

"I invited you," I replied, tucking my hair behind my ear.

"Oh," Tim said.

"Yeah, I wanted to share a few things with you that I never had the chance to. Would that be all right?" I felt awkward, as some things are more challenging to say.

"Sure. Go ahead. I think I have plenty of time to hear things these days!" Tim laughed, making light of his afterlife.

"OK, well, here it goes. I wanted to tell you how much I looked up to you when I was little, how much I wished to be your little sister, and truly, how much I longed to be your friend. But things got complicated in our childhood home, where our parents' erratic behavior drove us apart, especially as we grew older."

"Yeah, tell me about it. Living in that house was a minefield," Tim agreed.

"Tim, when they seated us at the kitchen table every night and berated us for not being the people they wanted us to be ... my heart would break every time I looked up through my tears and saw you slumped over and sobbing. I wanted to scream at them and tell them to *stop it*. Stop it for you. And stop it for me. But I couldn't. And you couldn't. They would have killed us."

I locked eyes with him. "Tim, I wanted to tell you how sorry I am for what happened to you."

Tim stood up and looked out over the hills. "When I was alive, I should have sought help for all the trauma of my youth. Yes, including being relinquished and adopted. I didn't know how to ask for help. Do you remember how Dad said I wasn't 'man enough' throughout my life? How was I supposed to ask for help and risk sounding weak?" Tim's voice trembled.

"And that's just the thing: you couldn't have. Neither could I. Asking for help would have exposed what Mom and Dad did to us in that house. We had to stay silent to survive," I agreed. "I wish we could have been there for each other, able to confide in one another. But it was too risky. You never knew whose side I was on, and I didn't know the same about you."

"I wish that, too. It was lonely. I wasn't ever able to get out from underneath those crushing feelings. I wish we could have been there for one another; it probably would have made a huge difference," Tim said.

"I'd like to be here for each other now. Are you OK with that?" I said, smiling at my brother, knowing this would be the first conversation of many we would have at The Gathering Place.

9

All is Not Well

The final years of my parents' lives were just as chaotic and confusing as their earlier years. Staying at home to pass away is not as desirable as it may seem. This is true for older people experiencing it, as well as the caregivers, and others trying to manage their needs.

A home is not a hospital and does not have the staff and tools necessary to ensure safety and provide proper medical care. However, I helped transform the once picturesque ranch-style home where my parents had lived for 50 years into a medical facility: they both wore hospital gowns, slept in hospital beds in safety-proofed rooms, and the seven-foot traditional dining room table was cluttered with medications and lifesaving equipment. A ramp had been power-drilled and bolted into the expensive marble foyer floor, and the new "furniture" included wheelchairs, oxygen tanks, and an electric Hoyer lift for transfers. And, of course, morphine in the refrigerator.

I still lived in the same city as my parents, and I offered to support them during this time in their lives. It had been their wish to die in their own home, the house where I had grown up and a place where I had suffered immensely. They often asked if I would move in after their death, and my answer was always a firm "*no*." They never appeared curious or asked me about it further.

Their final years coincided with the coronavirus pandemic. The inability to go anywhere except for urgent trips to the emergency room made it particularly challenging, as it was unsafe for us to travel freely. It softened the blow for them to be homebound since the world was in a similar situation.

Tim had moved to Golden, Colorado, with two of his adult children in 2010. They shared a couple of duplexes he inherited from our grandparents. Tim had not visited Tulsa since our parents' 60th wedding anniversary in 2017. Despite having suffered a mild heart attack just six months earlier and undergoing a stent procedure to improve blood flow, my mother had judged him harshly for not visiting.

"He's just dead to me. And no, I don't want to talk to him if he calls. I have *nothing* to say to him!" my mother would say. She didn't realize then that she would indeed never speak with him again.

Tim's youngest daughter called me in the early morning hours of July 27, 2020, to tell me her father had died of cardiac arrest. Her words made no sense to me. Trying to comprehend, I said, *"Wait … what? My brother died last night?"*

It fell to me to deliver this devastating, incomprehensible news. Accompanied by my daughter, Dana, who had returned to Tulsa after her college campus had shut down due to the pandemic, we went to my parents' home together.

Dana is wise beyond her years, and her presence steadied me in those moments, as always. She offered so much love and support while I was trying to keep my parents alive and somewhat happy. My daughter is one of my life's most significant and cherished gifts.

My parents couldn't understand me while I was wearing a mask, so I removed it despite the risk of exchanging germs. After much repetition, the message got through, and once they understood that their son had died, silence fell over the room.

Tim had been the father of five now-adult children, four of them quadruplets. There is no doubt that their father, the brother I was raised with, had passed away far too soon at 60 years old. Several years earlier, Tim and his wife underwent a bitter divorce, prompting him to relocate to Golden, Colorado, where he secured a position as a technical services specialist for a company in downtown Denver. Weeks had passed since my father and Tim last spoke on the phone, and it had been far longer since my mother had talked to him.

Now that Dana was back in Tulsa, rather than State College, Pennsylvania, she and I went grocery shopping for her grandparents every week, often several times.

Sometimes, we had to visit three or four stores to meet all their needs and demands.

My mother would say things like, "Emma, no, no, this isn't right! I wanted the *peach-flavored* oatmeal! Not this kind!"

It was almost impossible to explain to my homebound parents what it was like outside because of the pandemic shutdown. I took a deep breath and explained to her once more that the grocery store shelves were empty. We were fortunate to find *any* oatmeal or even toilet paper. She would look at me blankly, then shift her expression to *"I don't believe you."*

My poor mother, who had always taken pride in her appearance, slowly became deaf, then lost her ability to walk, and finally could no longer see. It was devastating for her. We consulted doctors who struggled to communicate the seriousness of her condition to her. Once you lose your eyesight and hearing, there's no way to regain them. The truth of these matters infuriated her. It must be incredibly difficult to endure these experiences—having no hope and knowing your body is shutting down. I think it's especially hard when that's what you've valued most in life rather than seeing these final days as a chance to connect with loved ones and say meaningful goodbyes. Perhaps even to find peace by seeking reconciliation, offering honest apologies, and making amends.

"I regret hitting my son one time when he was growing up," I overheard my mother say sorrowfully in her kitchen to one of the many caregivers who had come and gone. She often unburdened her soul to some caregivers who professed to be Christian in faith, hoping they would absolve her of her guilt.

With my back to them, I froze at her words.

Once? She admitted to hitting my brother once. And what about the hundreds of times you hit me?

I couldn't breathe. The familiar sensation of my throat constricting and the rush of all my past traumas pooling in my esophagus paralyzed me. I had been conditioned to stifle my emotions to escape my parents' punitive reactions. Flashes of memories of my mother's unbridled anger, which led her to hit both my brother and me throughout our childhood, punched me in the gut. I wanted to scream as I recalled the last vicious slaps she had dealt me in that very kitchen when I was 17.

"Do you think God will forgive me?" my mother asked in a small, childlike voice. I recognized this tone because she often used it when seeking sympathy. The new caregiver, an evangelical Christian, seemed more than ready to tell her that God forgave her.

The caregiver said what my mother wanted to hear: "God knows your heart. He knows you're sorry."

My thoughts, filled with righteous anger, resounded in my head, *"But does He? Are you sure He knows you're sorry? And by the way, the Holy Mystery is NOT a he!"*

~

When I accepted the job of helping my parents stay in their home rather than following their doctor's recommendation to move to assisted living, I had no idea what lay ahead for us all. It became five years of uncertainty.

Between getting them safely to doctors, obtaining the necessary medications and blood work, making their home safe enough to live in, taking them to the emergency room after numerous falls, and managing the hiring, oversight, and termination of various caregiver agencies—along with the rest of the list that's too long to recount—I found myself held captive by them once again. My daughter and I were both consumed and overwhelmed by their endless needs. That might have all been manageable if not for the most critical factor. Despite the heroic efforts my daughter and I made to help them stay in their home until they passed, they remained discontent. Bitterly discontent. And hateful.

"Where have you been?! You have no idea how bored I am. What have you been up to, anyway?" my mother exclaimed one day as Dana and I walked in with all the groceries, medications, and other items we had ordered, coordinated, and picked up for them.

"Mom, I was out getting your medications. The pharmacy needed approval from your doctor, who forgot to send the prescriptions for fulfillment. I then bought your new walker—purple, just as you wanted. After that, I had to return Dad's damaged wheelchair. All those things took time!" I was weary as I stood in front of my mother. She was sitting in the new, top-of-the-line lift chair I had bought and set up for her.

She hesitated. My gut twisted. I had long ago learned

the signs of when she was about to deliver a symbolic slap across my face.

"So, how's your *little boyfriend?*" my mother spat. Her words struck me like a splash of icy water in the face.

"My what?" I asked in disbelief. She shot me a withering look—one I had come to expect from her. It always reminded me of the sneer from the green-skinned Wicked Witch of the West in the 1939 movie *The Wizard of Oz.*

"Your boyfriend! That's where you spend all your time instead of being with us," my mother declared as if it were the truth.

I was furious and barely able to respond. Her pronunciation of "boyfriend" felt malicious and shameful, and my cheeks felt ablaze.

"*As if,* Mom! As if I had time for a boyfriend! If I'm not here with you, Dana and I are out getting everything you and Dad need. We're doing our best! You're not giving me enough time to breathe life into my own!"

I was on the verge of angry tears that made me realize, once again, the sadness of accepting that she was who she was.

"Well, that figures. That you don't have a boyfriend. How will you ever get a man when your hair looks like that? That picture you showed me from the fancy gala looked like you'd just stepped out of the shower, for Christ's sake."

My eyes locked on hers.

"Mary! Come on, now. You don't mean that." My dad said in a half-hearted attempt to defend me.

"Now, don't get so sensitive like you always do, Emma. I'm just being honest," my mom said, defending herself without remorse.

"Yeah, Mom, I know. It's fine. You're just being honest."

Clearly, my mom and I had reached a new low in our tumultuous mother-daughter relationship. Her fragility and jealousy seemed limitless. As a child, she shamed me for missing and crying for a woman she claimed had "thrown me away like yesterday's trash." As a young teen and beyond, she treated me like the other woman in the house. *"Mirror, mirror, on the wall, who is the fairest of them all?"* She couldn't bear having an adopted Snow White living under her roof. However, it did make her forget all about trying to look and be praised for being a savior.

My mother's cutting comment, meant to shred my spirit, reminded me of the countless times she'd wielded her words and hands as weapons. Once, just before one of my high school singing performances, she acted determined to undermine my self-confidence by saying hurtful things while pretending to be concerned.

"Emma, are you leaving? What will you do about your face?" she asked, circling her hand in the air as if cleaning a window of dirt and grime.

Her remark froze me in my tracks just as I reached for the door handle to leave for the performance. My nerves about performing a solo were already at a high pitch, and as an ambivert, I only had enough energy to make it through the solo I had fought so hard to perform.

"What do you mean?" I regretted taking the bait the moment the words left my mouth. I was thinking, *"Just leave! This won't be good!"*

"You just don't look your best. Maybe we should see a dermatologist to have a look at that poor skin of yours."

I had a few pimples, but nothing a little concealer wouldn't cover. My new dress, heels, and long hair styled in soft curls made me feel beautiful. More noteworthy, I felt confident enough to stand in front of an audience. However, I also knew my mother's comments deflated me with each passing second.

"Gee, thanks, Mom. Sorry you're not coming to hear me sing. At least Dad plans to be there. Maybe next time. I've gotta go …"

As I stepped out the door, I heard, "I can't say *anything* to you, *foolish girl*, without you acting absolutely *ridiculous*."

~

My elderly parents started experiencing accidents and falls. At one point, they both fell simultaneously, making round-the-clock caregivers essential. Each shift required two caregivers, as both needed hands-on care. There were now four caregivers in the house daily, and despite all the exposure to germs, neither of my parents contracted COVID-19. Dana, my son Trevor, and I wondered if it might have been more merciful for them to catch the virus. What we witnessed as my parents' bodies deteriorated, piece by piece, was that concurrently, their sense of entitlement, stemming from never having done the hard work to become better or at least "good enough" human beings, was like a living hell.

Dana and I had flown to Denver to attend Tim's memorial service at the Golden Cemetery in Colorado. It had been a year and a half since Tim had passed, and only now, after production delays and a lack of workers during the COVID-19 pandemic, was Tim's headstone ready. Just before we headed out to Denver, I had spoken with my father about my mom's daily care at home. She had been bedridden for months and required constant attention. Caregivers struggled to meet her basic needs, often performing their duties without privacy. As her digestive system slowed, she experienced significant pain. Each time caregivers attempted to change or move her to prevent additional bedsores, she would cry out in agony. It was terrible for her and distressing to watch, as we felt powerless to offer anything other than emotional support.

My dad was deeply affected by watching his extremely modest wife undergo undignified and distressing procedures to assist her bodily functions. The anxiety caused his advanced Parkinson's disease to worsen, with uncontrollable tremors and poor muscle coordination.

"Dad, I know you don't want to hear this, but I don't think we can continue to provide Mom with the care she needs at home." I waited silently, hoping he would hear my words.

Amazingly, he didn't say no. By then, I had been playing doctor for several years. I had learned to manage over 15 prescriptions between them, including breathing treatments and five different glaucoma eye drops, which cost $350 per bottle. I also scheduled doctor appointments for eye injections for macular degeneration, maintained the yard and house, and handled financial matters.

Narcotics sometimes went missing, and caregivers never seemed to know where they had gone; it was often up to my discretion to "guess" the amount to give to them, as well as keep track of drugs that had caused severe adverse reactions, yet the doctor continued to prescribe. There was no regulating authority, no primary doctor, and no comprehensive treatment plan for my parents and their well-being. It appeared that there was no end in sight to this insane nightmare we were experiencing.

Dana and I returned to Tulsa just two days before my mom's passing. Upon our arrival, the hospice team said the moment had come to administer the morphine that had been in the refrigerator for months. Stroking my mom's silver hair as I stood by her hospital bed in her once-lovely garden room, which had always been the gathering place of the home, I told her I had a sponge on a stick for her to suck on. It looked like a lollipop.

As I gently placed it into her mouth, she said, "Why do I always feel so bad?" My heart squeezed as I remembered her often feeling poorly. It was more than most people seemed to experience, and I had no answer for her.

Dana and Trevor rushed over after I called to tell them I was reasonably sure it was time for goodbyes. Together, we spent my mom's last afternoon with her. She was mostly sedated and spoke very little. It felt as though we were witnessing my mother's transition. I was losing another mother. My birth mother had passed away just weeks after Tim's fatal heart attack. And I learned that my birth father had also passed just the year before. It struck me that I was about to have only one living parent, my dad.

As I stood by my mom's hospital bed in my childhood home, my mind wandered, reflecting on our stormy relationship. I felt the weight of the abuse she inflicted on me, yet I understood that it was her only way of loving others. She never seemed capable of loving in a manner that captured the true essence of love. The little affection she offered often brought pain. Despite her treatment of me and others, I still didn't wish for her to experience such a sad final exit. I always imagined, or perhaps fantasized, that she would apologize to me just before her death and grow a heart in the face of her mortality.

I then pondered: Would that have been enough for me? A sincere apology? Admission of guilt? Maybe. I've forgiven her, nonetheless, not as someone who deserved it but as someone who I've accepted allowed a deep-seated meanness to consume her. I grieve the person she might have been.

If I've learned anything, it's that resisting reality prolongs the pain. Acceptance of what we cannot change is essential. For my mom to acknowledge the suffering and anguish she'd caused me since the day she brought me into her home as an infant born of another woman, she would have needed to be someone entirely different.

The caregiver on duty called me at 3:00 a.m., informing me that she had passed. I got dressed and drove the short two miles to where my lifeless mother lay in her hospital bed, covered with the purple velour comforter that Dana and I had bought for her. I had always known death was near, but when it finally came, it still enveloped me in profound shock and sadness.

I had been sitting at the family kitchen table since 3:45 a.m., talking with the hospice team, and had called the funeral home. It struck me deeply that I was once again informing a family member about the passing of a loved one.

Around 7:00 a.m., I quietly opened the door to my brother's old room, where my dad had been sleeping since my mom had pushed him out of their bedroom two years prior, claiming that their king-sized bed wasn't large enough for them both. My dad had acquiesced. I protested but declared I would buy him a new mattress since they hadn't replaced it since my brother left for college more than 40 years ago.

"Dad," I whispered, gently touching his shoulder. I paused, hearing my voice, which sounded so young.

"Dad," I said a bit louder, giving him another gentle shake.

"Whaaaat?" he said, attempting to emerge from a deep sleep. He moaned, coughed, and then tried to focus on me.

I gave him a moment longer before I found the words and choked back tears to say, "Dad, Mom passed away last night."

"Oh, nooo! No. No." My dad cried as he buried his face in his hands and shook his head in despair.

10

A Sad Ending

My mom's passing caused my dad to sink into a deeper level of depression, one that seemed to amplify his feelings of entitlement. Even more bizarre was his behavior and comments, which suggested he believed I would become his new wife, often referring to me by my mom's name, Mary. It was heart-wrenching when I had to draw a boundary and tell him I couldn't plan his every meal, be at his home constantly, or serve as his sole source of entertainment. Hearing my words infuriated him, but I stood firm. I clarified that I would do my best, but I also needed to care for my own responsibilities and health.

"Dad, if you moved to assisted living, like some of your other friends, you'd have much more to do than you do here at home. I know plenty of caregivers are always here, but it's not the same as having activities and friends to share them with." I had said these words to both my parents whenever they complained about how bored they were. Yet, I faced the same resistance each time.

"No! I'm going to die in my own home, goddammit! Don't ever talk about that again!"

"OK, Dad. But what I mean is that I can't be your everything. I'm running ragged here."

"*Fine*. Go live your own life. *Shit*. Just forget about me and be sure to go and have a good time," my dad said, turning his head away from me.

My exhaustion was genuine. I endlessly discussed the stress I felt with my mental health counselors. Each week, I attended my sessions feeling drained and confused about how to manage keeping my parents alive, and then, just my father. My highly qualified, ethical, and competent counselors also addressed the fact that I had agreed to care for people who had treated me cruelly in my youth and still often did. My parents were both in denial about their lives ending and how they relied on me to prevent the inevitable from happening. I felt like I was dancing as fast and furiously as I could, while my parents seemed unaware that their choice to die at home was causing an immense amount of mental and physical stress to others in our family—mainly to Dana and me. Without my therapists and the support of my adult children, I wouldn't have survived those challenging years.

Another important thing I did to stay sane during those arduous years was to begin writing my story, which evolved into *The Gathering Place: An Adoptee's Story*, followed by *A Fire Is Coming*. Every day, I wrote, even after chaotic days of taking my parents to doctors, picking up medications, or hiring a new caregiver agency after needing to terminate the previous one. Writing became my medicine; the words flowed effortlessly from me onto the paper. However, a part of me still felt frightened to let my parents know I was writing my story.

In fact, I was petrified. I took precautions to ensure they would *not* find out. I even created a persona, Emma Stevens (the surname Stevens reflects my adoration for Samantha Stephens from the 1960s television show *Bewitched*), to self-publish my two memoirs. I did this not only to protect the identities of everyone in my book but mainly because my younger self still could not bear the sense of deprivation I would have felt if my parents discovered it, leaving no time for repair.

Amazingly, after establishing a strong social media presence and appearing as a guest on numerous podcasts, my parents never learned about my books. It's ironic to recall my mother's words from many years ago when I was a child: "You'd better not go writing a book someday about how we abused you."

While I was writing, my daughter was working on her dissertation for her doctoral program. I was amazed that she could help me address her grandparents' needs while staying on track to graduate as a Doctor of Communications and support me in maintaining my sanity.

In the fall of 2022, even my dad's beloved obsession with watching football could not comfort him. He would growl, hiss, and pout when Dana and I visited him daily. He blamed me for his situation and for not dancing quickly enough for him. It was increasingly difficult to want to spend time with him. I often felt guilty leaving his home, especially when I found him asleep and didn't want to wake him. I would sigh in relief as I felt the tension in my shoulder and neck muscles gradually release while I quietly slipped out of his house for a few hours of freedom.

After dinner with him one night, as Dana, Trevor, and I did two or three nights a week, he called me Mary again and said he needed to talk with me.

"Sure. What is it, Dad?" I stood up from my chair at the kitchen table and moved closer to him so he could hear me better.

"Why do you keep talking about needing to go *home*?" His words hung in the air, and I tried to make sense of them.

"Well, Dad, I've been gone all day, and my cats are probably hungry! You know what I mean?" I was hoping to see if this answered his question or not.

He huffed, "Mary, *this is* your goddamn home! Why do you always talk about needing to go *home*?"

"Dad … my name is Emma. I'm your daughter, and I love you. This is Dana, your granddaughter, and she loves you, too. Trevor is your grandson. I haven't lived here in decades, but I come over every day—sometimes twice daily." As the words left my mouth, I realized my dad was showing clear signs of dementia, and it was becoming harder to ignore. What I wasn't prepared for, however, was the escalating intensity of his anger, which had been appearing more frequently. A common symptom of dementia.

I realized a little too late that he would not understand my explanation and that it would have been more compassionate of me to say, "I'm just going out for a while. I'll be right back, Dad."

Dana and I took his grocery list and noticed a significant change. Formerly, he had requested countless items such as meats, frozen dinners, and fruits, but now it listed only yogurt, Ensure, and Pedialyte.

After delivering these items, Dana and I entered a scene that a daughter and granddaughter should never have to witness. We walked into my dad's home, where the caregivers had him suspended in the air, cradled in a human-sized sling attached to the Hoyer lift that was used while changing his bedsheets. My once robust, energetic, and often brutish bullying father suddenly seemed small, docile, and as helpless as a baby. I was highly concerned about the caregivers' ability to properly operate the lift machine and prevent my dad from crashing onto the tile floor. After assuring me they knew how to manage the machine and that it was safe and efficient, I reluctantly agreed that somehow his sheets needed to be changed.

Within six months of my mom's passing, my dad was now confined to a hospital bed in the family garden room, just as my mom had been. It had become too risky for the caregivers to continue transferring him from his lift chair to his bed using the Hoyer machine. Although the caregivers assured me that his vital signs were stable, the levels of pain medication and his Parkinson's both affected his ability to communicate and created new neurological complications.

I felt sad when my dad's lucid moments began to fade into nothingness. However, I was able to express my love for him without him being combative or blaming me for his unhappiness. Now, when I visited him, I could tell him how much I would miss him—the dad I played with in the ocean so long ago—not the abusive dad. I would stroke his hair, lightly kiss his forehead, and place my hand over his heart, rubbing it in a soothing, circular motion as I told him how much I loved him. Those were precious moments for me and ones I will never forget. I like to think that my dad was aware, even though he couldn't speak, enough to feel the love I showed him as I expressed how much I would miss him.

Just as life is often a both/and experience, his subdued state allowed me to express how angry and sad I had been all my life because he never protected me. I told him that he was abusive and narcissistic and that his love hurt almost as much as my mother's. Their fear of scarcity led both my mom and my dad to try their best to keep me in a kind of bondage that left me feeling oppressed and unable to breathe.

When my dad passed away, he was not in his home as he had wished. The last twelve hours of his life were spent in a skilled care facility. The hospice team and the caregiver agency blamed each other for the improper care of my father. This disagreement resulted in both telling me they could no longer care for him at home.

He would have to go to a skilled care facility.

My heart squeezed with despair. I had no choice but to agree to the immediate transfer of my father to a place where he would receive better care. After he had settled into his new room, I approached him and ran my hand over his light brown and gray hair. I placed my hand on his chest and whispered that I'd return in the morning. He was in a deep sleep and did not respond. I hoped he'd heard me anyway.

Later that day, Dana and I retrieved some personal belongings from his house to bring to him. As we walked through the kitchen, we noticed the caregiver who had stayed behind to help take family pictures out of their frames was sitting on the kitchen floor, hunched over, with her legs sprawled out, appearing as though she might be sick.

I rushed to her, placing my hand on her shoulder. She slowly rose to her feet and began telling us that she was all right but was emotional about my dad. I hugged her. Sensing she felt better, I went into the house to collect my dad's things.

"Mom, do you know what she was doing?!" Dana asked me as we walked down the long hallway of my parents' home. The home once held many family photos, but the walls were now bare, leaving me with a hollow feeling and a sense of lost chapters and lives coming to an end. I had decided to begin packing the house for when I eventually sold it.

"What do you mean?" I asked.

"Mom, she was '*huffing*!'"

"What?" I had no idea what that meant.

Suddenly, I remembered when a caregiver confessed to me that my parents' pool maintenance worker had attempted to sell meth to her in our family's driveway. Situations like missing medications, selling narcotics, and even having to prosecute a caregiver who stole my mom's debit card for sending herself money through an online cash application were strange yet regular occurrences.

"It's when you inhale things to get high—like aerosols, markers, and nail polish removers. Didn't you see the empty compressed air cans in her purse scattered all over the floor? She was drooling!" Dana was both concerned for the caregiver and horrified. Of all days for something like this to happen!

Earlier, before transferring my father to the skilled care center, we also had to re-home my parents' beloved dogs. As an adoptee, the idea and necessity of re-homing anything is gut-wrenching. And for all intents and purposes, hadn't I been forced to re-home my father that very same day?

The next day, Dana's doctoral program's graduation ceremony was scheduled, and we had planned to fly to Pennsylvania to attend. However, that did not happen.

Before leaving my father in the care of the doctors and nurses at the facility, I asked the head nurse if it was a good idea for me to leave town the next day due to my dad's health status. She assured me that his vitals were stable and not a concern. She advised Dana and me to proceed with our plans.

I called the facility early the following day to check on my dad. They informed me that it was breakfast time and all the staff were busy.

Minutes later, at 8:11 a.m., my cell phone rang.

"Hello, Emma. This is Randy from the hospice team. I regret to inform you that your father passed away this morning."

A chill ran through me. Had my dad already passed when I called eleven minutes earlier, and did they only check on him because of my call? For that matter, had he died right after I left him the evening before?

My dad had been taken from his home less than twelve hours earlier, having missed dying in his own home by just a few hours.

The same shock and sadness enveloped me, along with the realization that I was now left without any living parent. My parents had always conditioned me to believe that I could never succeed in life without them; their narcissism had hobbled me.

Yet my healthier self said, "But you're free now!" Despite extensive emotional work through psychotherapy, I knew I still faced a steep climb ahead. There were parts of me that were so afraid of what might happen if I chose to let go that it felt like it was choking off my airways. I needed to update these younger, traumatized parts so that a *quiet mind could hear intuition over fear.*

11

At the Pool

"OK, Tabitha! Your turn!" Athena and Justice stood at the far end of the small pool, encouraging six-year-old Tabitha to leap off the low diving board into the refreshing water. I was right beside her. Tabby, Tabitha's cat, was nearby, chasing a yellow butterfly. I gently slipped into the water, hoping to show Tabitha I would be there for her.

"I can do it! I know I can! Watch me, everyone!" Before Tabitha finished her shout, she raced down the board and, without hesitation, made a small jump into the pool's deep end. Her splash was as tiny as she was, yet her courage was enormous. From that moment on, she repeated her heroic jumps off the board again and again.

I joined Athena and Justice at a small table by the pool, watching and encouraging Tabitha as she continued to show off for us. It was a joy to see her and to remember being her during those times in her life—our life—when she didn't have to bear the heavy cloak of fear and sadness that she often wore at home.

"Hey, when is Mallory coming? Didn't you say she might?" Tabitha had briefly met Mallory the last time she visited The Gathering Place. Both Tabitha and Mallory began to visit more often as they felt increasingly relaxed and enjoyed being there.

The addition of the pool at The Gathering Place brought me joy. My happiest childhood memories were swimming, diving, and playing with my cat Tabby. I was about to answer Tabitha when she submerged herself underwater. We all hoped to see Mallory again. I was greatly encouraged by her more frequent visits and how, each time, she seemed less hypervigilant.

Tabitha's head emerged from the water, and she instantly raised her arms high into the air, calling out, "Mallory! Over here!" We turned to see sweet Mallory slowly reaching the pool's edge.

She bent down and stuck her hand in the water, declaring, "It's too cold."

"Maybe at first, but it warms up quickly. We'll all join you if you do, Mallory!" I stood up, removed the towel wrapped around me, and joined Tabitha. I also grabbed the Nerf ball for a fun game of catch in the pool. Mallory watched as I sat on the edge of the pool and then slowly slipped into the water. I turned and reached my hand out, saying, "See, it's not so bad. You'll get used to it in seconds! Come play with us!"

"I should be getting back. My mommy and daddy

would be weally mad if they knew I was here." Mallory looked uncomfortable and was shaking. In distress, she backed away from the pool's edge and rubbed her brow. I quickly swam back to the cement edge of the pool and stretched my arms out flat, feeling the sun's warmth through my outstretched limbs.

I looked at her intently. "Mallory, I need to tell you something. There was a time when you had to fear what your parents might do to you, but that's not something you need to worry about anymore. You survived those dark days—it's over now. You, Tabitha, and the rest of us are free. I will help you understand that you no longer need to feel afraid." Mallory's brow softened as she looked at me with curiosity, unsure how to respond.

"Mal-lor-eey! Jump in!" Tabitha squealed, joyfully splashing her hands and arms in the water.

Mallory couldn't resist; after quickly removing her oversized T-shirt, she eased into the pool's shallow end. Once the water reached her belly, Mallory inched beneath the surface. The two girls swam toward each other and embraced, laughter and giggles overwhelming them. They began diving underwater and shooting up as if fired from a cannon, bursting into another fit of laughter.

"Hey, catch!" I tossed the Nerf ball to Mallory. She caught it but then dropped it. After splashing around to retrieve it, she turned and threw the soaked ball to Justice, who passed it to Athena.

"Justice, whoa, easy there! You don't have to throw it like a bullet!" Athena laughed so hard that it was pointless to try to scold Justice.

"Oh, sorry!" Justice managed to say between her laughter.

"Here, catch, Tabitha!"

We continued to toss the ball to one another, splashing even more water out of the pool as we played. On a sunny day at The Gathering Place, we felt free.

Hours passed. The gang grew tired and crawled out of the pool one by one. We each found our towels and relaxed, letting the sun warm and toast our bodies. The cool breeze made the sun's rays feel even more delectable.

I positioned my towel between Tabitha's and Mallory's. Justice and Athena were a few towels away and appeared to have fallen asleep. Mallory sat up, brushed her wet and tangled hair from her face, and glanced at Tabitha.

"Are you ascared anymore, Tabtha?" Mallory struggled to pronounce Tabitha's name correctly. "You know, of getting in twouble?"

I lay down, curious about how Tabitha would respond. I didn't have to wait long before Tabitha sat up and draped herself over my belly to reply to Mallory, "I've been really ascared, too, but I believe Emma. She says it's all over now, that we've kinda been frozen in time, and that Emma is us now—but all growed up! Crazy, huh?"

Tabitha crossed her eyes to emphasize her point. The young girls giggled together, and I couldn't help but smile and chuckle softly. Hearing them figure things out made my heart feel like melted gold.

"Mallory, it's so much fun here! I hope you come a lot more. At first, I only came sometimes, but now I'm here almost every day! Emma and the others take great care of me. They brush my hair, let me sit in their laps, and they look after Tabby cat, too!" Tabitha's face lit up as brightly as the sun's rays on her lightly freckled cheeks.

"Emma, tell her! Tell her how we've been telling ourselves a story that isn't even true, how we were never bad at all! And that Mommy and Daddy had broken things inside them…" Tabitha said the last part more softly, glancing at me to step in.

"Yeah, Tabitha is right. My parents," I paused and corrected myself, "*our* parents chose not to be kind people for most of their lives. It was paramount to them to make their version of the story correct. Although they 'loved' us in their way, it wasn't the true meaning of love. Love involves nurturing and wanting everyone you care for to be free. They had us—you, me, and the other parts of us—buy into a false narrative to manipulate and deceive us into serving them, making them feel better about themselves. The story was, 'We are your saviors, and you are here to honor us.'"

Mallory sat beside me, rocking herself with her knees tightly tucked to her chest. "I just want to be a good girl. I hate me for not making Mommy and Daddy happy. My other mommy and daddy left and never came back. What if they leave me, too?" Tears streamed down Mallory's face.

As I sat up to face her, I gathered my thoughts. "You can't hate yourself into becoming a better person." Her sorrowful eyes met mine. "I understand that this was how our parents controlled our behavior for their own benefit—but it was killing us!"

Now awake, Athena and Justice moved their towels closer to Mallory, Tabitha, and me.

Mallory shot them both a look. "I wemember you two! You used to get me in twuble!" Mallory's once-bent knees and tiny legs shot straight, and her fists clenched. "You made my mommy and daddy weal mad! I tried everything to *hide from you* so they'd be nice and love me."

Hearing Mallory's words felt like a horrific wind tunnel inside me, transporting me back to when I was three years old, the first time my mom told me I was adopted. I had reacted to her matter-of-fact announcement by sobbing uncontrollably. This caused her to become irate, claiming she had given me everything. Confused, I asked, "But what happened to her? Where is she now? Does she know I'm OK?" My mind, at three years old, was filled with concern for a mother who had given birth to me but was now nowhere to be found.

"How can you cry for a woman who threw you away?! You'd probably be in a gutter if it weren't for your father and me. We saved you. You and your brother Tim are selfish and ungrateful! Just wait until I tell your father how ridiculous you're acting! Go to your room. I can't stand to look at you right now." With that, my mother left me in tears and stomped away, slamming the door.

My curiosity often made my home life more volatile. *Curiosity*, which I refer to as Athena, had to be concealed—told to hide. She was not welcome in my adoptive home, especially when it came to asking questions about my adoption story.

My thoughts suddenly shifted to the 12-year-old part of myself. Justice, who is as bold and courageous as Athena, was also banned from my adoptive home because she disrupted my efforts to maintain peace at all costs. She was anything but a peacekeeper. Justice was always present but rarely free to express her thoughts, especially her strong will.

One day in August, my parents informed Tim and me that we were moving to a new city and school just one week before the move. I was just about to start Fifth Grade, and this shift meant we would be registering late at the new school. The school assigned me to an underachiever class, not considering my straight-A background and need for challenge. Among the ten fifth-grade classes sorted by achievement levels, the school placed me in the second-to-lowest class, the only class the registrar's office stated had room for a new student.

Justice boldly approached each of my parents, pleading that the new school was making a mistake. My parents repeatedly replied, *"Who do you think you are, Emma?* Don't rock the boat. We don't want to tell the school how to run things."

Most of my younger parts, particularly Mallory and Tabitha, had yet to find their voice. But Justice did. And

Athena did, too. This injustice ignited a rage within me. Not only did my parents appear indifferent to the fact that I had lost my home, friends, a neighborhood school, and challenging schoolwork—they allowed their daughter to be labeled by a school that employed a caste system, a label that would haunt me throughout my academic life. My parents should have advocated for me the way parents are supposed to. Justice and Athena, my parts that value truth above all else, scheduled an appointment with the school principal, believing I could rectify the mistake, but I was mistaken. The principal offered no assistance, and I remained in the same class. This oversight by my parents and the school happened again in my sixth-grade year.

Sadly, my parents' abandonment of me at 12 years old taught me to abandon myself. I often felt my reality vastly differed from what I perceived as the consensus reality. It was crazy-making. Yet, Justice and Athena stayed with me anyway, coming out when the oppression of life became too overwhelming.

Returning to Mallory, Tabitha, Justice, and Athena as we sat on our towels by the pool, I said, "I want to take this moment … and Mallory and Tabitha, please listen … I want to thank Justice and Athena for their courage and bravery. We might not have made it through our younger years without their resilience and tenacity."

I paused, then looked at Mallory and Tabitha, saying, "Also, a huge thank you goes to you and the other parts of us that kept us safe and out of harm's way as much as possible. You protected us in countless ways and helped us endure experiences akin to those of Dante's Inferno from 'The Divine Comedy.'"

"What's dat?" Mallory said, her face scrunched up.

"I'm sorry, little one! It's a story of a man named Dante who travels through the many challenges of what it means to be human. What I mean is that you're very strong and did a wonderful job protecting us. What if I told you that you have a different role now? You did your part perfectly, and now your job is to relax and have fun!"

"*NOOO!* My job is to make sure Mommy and Daddy don't leave me!" Mallory tensed her body as she leaned toward me, her eyes wide like an owl's.

"But you did it! The 'all-clear' trumpet has sounded, which means the war is over. You were a good and faithful soldier fighting a war you should never have had to endure. Our parents never abandoned us. They neglected us in other ways, but they never rehomed us like some adoptees sadly are." I paused to take a deep breath. "You protected us in the best ways you knew during that time in our lives, but we've grown up now. Many things you did back then to keep us safe now harm us."

Tabitha and Mallory exchanged glances.

Quickly, Tabitha turned her head toward me, her long, light brown ponytail trailing behind her. "But … what is our job now?" I sensed the unease in Tabitha and Mallory—their anxiety about letting go of thoughts, beliefs, and behaviors they had always regarded as true or necessary for their safety.

"That's the beauty of being at The Gathering Place! I've invited you all here to update you on things you might not know, especially to let you know that *I'm* your parent now, and I promise to treat you with love and respect. I love you in the truest sense of the word, which means I want freedom for all of us."

The moment brightened when our cat, Tabby, made biscuits on Mallory's towel with her paws, purring loudly like a motor. Tabitha let her finish, then picked her up, saying, "Look at Tabby's cute black-toe beans!" The two young ones showered Tabby with affection and cuddles.

"I'd love to hear your thoughts on what we've been talking about, Mallory," I said, returning the focus to the conversation. She paused as if pondering a profound question.

Looking up with her clear, bright blue-green eyes, she exclaimed, "I'm hungry!"

I suppressed the urge to shout *"Hallelujah!"* because I've come to understand that hunger returns once hypervigilance fades. When I'm in fight or flight, as if running from a bear, my nervous system thinks of one thing–RUN! But when entering the rest and digest mode, things like food sound enticing again. Mallory's statement also warmed me, as she might as well have said that she feels safe.

Instead, I replied, *"Excellent! Let's eat!"*

12

Integrity vs. Fragility

"Mary, where's your goddamn ring!" my father shouted at my mom.

"Stop yelling, Arthur! I left it inside. I'll go get it," Mom said as she returned to the house they had custom-built almost 50 years earlier.

"As well, you better! That ring cost me plenty. You'd think you'd take better care of a five-carat diamond wedding ring," he said, disgusted.

My parents bought the new wedding ring to replace her original one after "their ship came in." They both loved the statement it conveyed—declaring a sense of personal worth and success based on the size of the diamond. Ironically, it didn't fit her finger. The round-shaped solitaire ring was top-heavy. Due to its size and shape, the diamond would slide from side to side on her finger. To try to prevent that from happening, they had the jeweler place ridges inside the gold setting. It didn't work.

After my parents passed away, I included my mom's wedding ring in the estate sale. However, diamond experts who evaluated the ring for cut, color, clarity, and carat informed me that its classification was low-quality and worth very little. My parents had bought it for size alone, not for quality. I found this symbolic of their mindset and how they chose to live their lives. They nurtured their fragility instead of ever seeking integrity.

The irony of my parents claiming to want to raise two children from unknown origins, whom they regarded as coming from inferior backgrounds, is that they did so while ignoring and refusing to acknowledge our past. They disregarded and dishonored both me and my brother by not allowing us to grieve the loss of our first families or to recognize how that would shape us. If they could simply silence our selfish, ungrateful questions, those questions wouldn't exist. They would simply "forget" we were adopted, pretending we were their own creation. Allowing us space to explore that part of ourselves would only anger them and increase their fragility. Thus, one of the reasons for their purchasing us would be tarnished, leaving them with buyer's remorse.

To be fair, I believe my parents, both only children, needed to adopt children to create the perfect family and ensure someone would take care of them in their old age. My dad had a childhood with an enmeshed relationship with his mother and was emotionally neglected and possibly physically abused by his father. This shaped him to have a deep need to be in control, be revered, and have a sense of power. My mother lost her father to divorce in infancy and was raised by her mother and three maternal aunts who never had children of their own. They collectively raised my mother with excessive attention and without healthy boundaries that could help her outgrow childhood narcissism. My mother's father moved to another state to create a new family, whom she rarely saw due to the distance. Much like my father, I believe my mother also had abandonment issues related to an absent father.

Just as my parents chose to deny the flaws of the diamond, which they could only appreciate for its extravagant size, they were excited to have bought a boy and a girl to showcase as the family they had created. They just needed to continue to deny that their children had come from unknown sources and had a completely unrelated past. Truth seemed to be only an illusion to them.

In her 2021 book, *The Way of Integrity: Finding the Path to Your True Self,* Martha Beck states, "Integrity is the cure for unhappiness." This resonates with me. I now realize that I feel profoundly unhappy when I drift away from integrity and abandon my deep sense of truth. Not accepting my present reality can heighten my suffering. I've also learned that accepting my reality is significantly different from resigning myself to fate or justifying traumatic experiences. Acceptance always involves living in the present moment and taking the next best step toward health. Conversely, resigning myself to situations without addressing them can only lead to more suffering.

I learned these concepts from the Twelve-Step Program of Alcoholics Anonymous (AA) and Adult Children of Alcoholics & Dysfunctional Families (ACoA). For decades, I had resisted my reality, both consciously and unconsciously. However, drinking excessively to distract me from my pain and suffering finally brought me to my knees, presenting me with a fork in the road. I had to accept either that I had a problem far more significant than myself or that I might face an early death like my brother, Tim. I underwent a paradigm shift away from abandoning myself, which caused a change in my brain structure. I came to learn that drinking excessively affects areas of the brain that include the cerebral cortex and the hippocampus. "Shrinkage in these areas can lead to difficulties in learning new things, cause memory lapses, and can lead to dementia. However, continued abstinence can lead to ongoing improvements in cognitive functions, mood stability, and emotional well-being. Research shows that the brain can continue to heal for up to two years after quitting alcohol. During this time, the brain can regenerate new neurons and create new neural pathways, improving cognitive function, emotional regulation, and memory," says the National Institute on Alcohol Abuse and Alcoholism.

In 2016, I chose to start working through the steps of the Twelve-Step Program. I improved one step and one day at a time. I was determined to keep moving forward and accept my reality. I aimed to practice radical resilience and acceptance. These concepts helped me start discovering many other lessons in life and spiritual teachers who illuminated similar paths to health—paths that encouraged me to stop viewing life in a dualistic, status-quo manner.

Over eight years ago, I sat in an ACoA Twelve-Step meeting, feeling encouraged for starting my path to sobriety when I learned about the idea of becoming emotionally sober. I remember feeling as if I had been kicked in the stomach and thinking, "What? I have more work to do?!"

And yes, I began to realize I had overwhelming work ahead of me. Getting sober from alcohol was only the beginning of a much deeper journey. The realization of how much I needed to improve to become a better person for myself and others felt daunting. Practicing healthy boundaries, understanding my attachment style, and learning to regulate my emotions were all foreign concepts to me but were all part of the work I needed to do to achieve emotional sobriety. Abusing alcohol was only a symptom of my core issue. Until I uncovered the reasons behind my drinking, I was destined to repeat unhealthy patterns and seek out people, places, and things to soothe my unresolved trauma. Today, I view my sobriety as encompassing not only abstaining from alcohol but also refraining from all behaviors or thought patterns that do not promote health. Yelling at someone behind the counter in a store or being passive-aggressive with a friend are examples of a relapse in emotional health and sobriety.

The concept I've heard Richard Rohr discuss—that we are all addicted to our own way of thinking—resonates with me. He claims that "stinking thinking" is the universal addiction. He states, "Substance addictions like alcohol and drugs are merely the most visible form of addiction; in reality, we are all addicted to our habitual way of thinking and doing. These attachments are, at first, hidden to us. We cannot heal what we do not first acknowledge," writes Richard Rohr in *Breathing Under Water: Spirituality and the Twelve Steps*.

Gradually, my efforts to deconstruct, dismantle, and reevaluate my illusion of myself and everything I believed I knew began to bring me joy—joy I had never experienced before—along with peace I had never known. The more I opened myself to embrace the process, the more I began to feel a sense of completion. I found myself wanting more. My meditations included affirming to myself, "Yes, please, more of that!"

Although I knew I couldn't manifest my transformation, I felt that the more time I spent at The Gathering Place doing the hard work of self-reflection, the more awakened I became. Just as I abstained from alcohol, I also sought to rid myself of other blind spots. Blind spots (addictions) that included telling myself the false narrative of not being good enough.

One of my earliest awakenings happened during my senior year of college when I faced a challenging decision about whether to marry my college boyfriend. It was one of the first times I accepted my reality and realized that my discomfort stemmed from not admitting

I just wasn't ready for the commitment of marriage. Author Scott Peck's book, *The Road Less Traveled*, assisted me in my decision. The book presents concepts of confronting and solving problems that emphasize personal growth and spiritual development. It offers insights into confronting and overcoming challenges, as well as living a more fulfilling and meaningful life. The book profoundly affected me and provided my first taste of a spiritual awakening. During this time of practicing radical acceptance, I chose not to marry my fiancé.

However, my surge of clarity in college to follow the road less traveled was short-lived, replaced by my urge to follow fantasy. Nevertheless, the seed that would take root many years later had been planted.

13

Tools to Breathe

Over the years, I've experimented with countless healing modalities—some ancient, some modern, some deeply spiritual, and others more clinical or creative. Alcoholics Anonymous (AA) and Adult Children of Alcoholics (ACoA) have provided the foundational framework for my recovery, offering me structure, language, and community when I needed it most. However, healing is layered, and I've found that no single path holds all the answers. These additional tools became lifelines—each one offering a thread of hope, insight, or relief. I've read hundreds of books, tried various practices, and sought out what resonated most with my truth. Healing isn't linear, and what works for one person might not work for another. I'm sharing these not as prescriptions, but as possibilities—things that helped me reconnect with myself, breathe more deeply, and move forward with intention.

The Enneagram was one of the first tools that helped me hold compassion and curiosity about how I move through the world. It's a personality framework that identifies nine core types, each with motivations, fears, and behavior patterns, offering insight into how we relate to ourselves and others. Learning that I was a *Type Four—the Individualist*—explained so much: the longing, the emotional intensity, the desire to feel unique and deeply understood. More than that, it provided me with a roadmap, revealing my gifts and the patterns I fall into when I am stressed or disconnected from my truth. My favorite part of working with the Enneagram is that it doesn't box you in—it invites you to grow. It offers grace for where you are and vision for who you're becoming.

Internal Family Systems (IFS) transformed how I understand my inner world. It's a therapeutic model that sees the mind as distinct "parts," each with its role, emotions, and perspective, like little personalities within us. IFS helped me realize that the parts of me I once tried to silence—like the pleaser, protector, and angry one—were trying to help me survive. The real breakthrough came when I stopped judging those parts and started listening to them with compassion. It was like gathering all my inner voices around a table and learning that none of them were bad—they were just carrying burdens that needed to be acknowledged and gently released.

One of the most surprising breakthroughs in my healing came through a modality that didn't require endless talking: eye movement desensitization and reprocessing, or EMDR. Using bilateral stimulation, like tapping or guided eye movements, helped me reprocess traumatic memories without reliving them. What once felt like an emotional ambush began to lose its grip. I didn't have to narrate every detail; instead, I could feel the pain shift, settle, and finally rest in the past where it belonged.

One of the first ideas my therapist asked me to consider while preparing for my own EMDR work was to visualize a place where I could generate feelings of calm and safety internally. This serves as a relaxation technique to recall when needed. Coincidentally, I had just shown her an image I loved of a big, old oak tree with a rope-and-wood bench swing attached, growing on a green grassy hillside. I chose this image to represent my safe place and marked the beginning of what would evolve into regular visits and writings about my Gathering Place, which continue to this day. Combining EMDR work with IFS "parts" work has enabled me to write about my parts of self, get to know them, and create magic that is helping me find peace.

When I found myself trapped in thought spirals or reacting from a place of fear or shame, cognitive behavioral therapy provided me with practical tools. By identifying the distorted beliefs I had absorbed—like "I'm too much" or "Love equals abandonment"—and challenging them with gentler truths, I began to reclaim my narrative. It wasn't about pretending everything was fine; it was about noticing my thoughts, examining the evidence, and choosing new ones that aligned with who I was becoming.

I didn't have words for it then, but I lived most of my early life in what Carl Jung might call the False Self—the part of me shaped to survive, be acceptable, and keep the peace. Jung's concept of the True Self gave language and meaning to what I'd always sensed: that there was a deeper, more authentic me beneath all the adaptations. The journey back to her has been both painful and beautiful. It's like uncovering a forgotten song and learning to sing it again in my own voice.

Understanding the layered identity of being adopted became clearer when I discovered the Adoptee Consciousness Model by JaeRan Kim, PhD. It outlines the stages of awareness adoptees often navigate—from internalizing dominant narratives to reclaiming our own truths. What struck me most was the realization that questioning, grieving, and even feeling anger weren't signs of being ungrateful; they were signs of growth. This model validated much of my inner journey and reminded me that I wasn't alone in it.

Dr. Steven Hassan's BITE model—which focuses on controlling Behavior, Information, Thought, and Emotion—helped me identify something I had only felt as vague unease: how my autonomy had been systematically eroded. Although initially developed to understand cults and coercive control, the framework resonated deeply with my experience growing up in a family system that demanded obedience, silence, and self-erasure. Seeing it laid out in black and white was both chilling and liberating. It confirmed what I knew in my body but had struggled to articulate.

There's something deeply human about Erik Erikson's stages. They helped me trace the emotional map of growing up, especially the detours and unfinished chapters. "Identity versus role confusion," "Intimacy versus isolation" weren't just academic terms; they were real tensions I'd lived through. Seeing them spelled out helped me revisit each developmental season with greater gentleness, offering grace to the younger versions of myself who were doing their best with what they had.

I used to think Abraham Maslow's pyramid was just a classroom diagram, but it turned out to be a mirror. His Hierarchy of Needs showed me that our yearning to grow and create can only flourish when the foundation is solid—when we feel safe, connected, and seen. That realization reframed so much of my past. I wasn't failing to thrive; I was trying to bloom in drought. The idea of self-actualization became less about achievement and more about self-trust.

Spiral Dynamics provided me with a framework for understanding how individuals—and even entire societies—grow and evolve through various stages of consciousness. It helped me stop taking things so personally. I could see that not everyone operates from the same worldview or emotional maturity, and that's okay. It also prompted me to examine where I was getting stuck and where I could expand. It was less about judgment and more about awareness of myself, others, and the systems we live in.

Richard Rohr's framing of spiritual transformation through the lens of Order, Disorder, and Reorder gave shape to my chaos. His teachings helped me understand that disruption, which once felt like a personal failure or collapse, was often an invitation to a more profound clarity. The "Disorder" was not the end, but a necessary breaking open; a call for the walls of my world to expand. I started to see my life not as a series of missteps but as a sacred unfolding where each stage served a purpose. Ultimately, paradoxically, everything belongs and everything is connected.

Long before I could articulate it, I felt drawn to the radical heart of Jesus' Sermon on the Mount. His teachings on death and renewal—on letting go of ego, loving our enemies, and mourning as a pathway to blessing—offered me both challenge and comfort. What I once saw as religious platitudes, I now experience as profound psychological truths. It highlighted that beholding happens when we stop trying to "hold" and allow ourselves to "be held" by the other. We are completely enchanted by something outside and beyond ourselves. These teachings allowed me to hold grief and grace in the same breath.

Their quiet, steady invitation inward drew me to the yogic teachings. The journey toward complete enlightenment isn't about escaping pain or bypassing emotion—it's about sitting with all of it until the layers fall away. I resonated most with the emphasis on integration: breath, body, spirit, and awareness moving as one. It isn't about arriving at some perfect state but choosing presence repeatedly.

Most recently, I've discovered the helpful tool of aligning my energy by learning about the chakras. Chakra is a Sanskrit word that appeared thousands of years ago in Hindu texts, meaning "Wheel of Light." Later, the chakras showed up in the roots of yoga. The knowledge of this can affect your entire sense of well-being by living a balanced and harmonious life. "In general, the chakras are where we receive, assimilate, and distribute our life energies," states applied psychologist and yoga teacher Diane Malaspina, PhD. "The chakras are concentrated hubs or centers that align along the center of the body, from the base of the pelvic floor up to the crown of the head." While there are seven chakras, I was especially interested in the sacral and the throat chakras.

The sacral chakra, known as the second chakra, governs emotions, creativity, and self-acceptance. By learning to work with your sacral chakra, you can unlock a deeper connection to your most actual feelings, passions, and the beauty of the world around you.

The fifth chakra, the throat chakra, helps us express ourselves verbally. Physically, it influences the throat, vocal cords, mouth, tongue, and lymphatic system. When this chakra is balanced and in sync with the sacral chakra, you voice thoughts, feelings, and ideas accurately and clearly. When out of balance, the throat chakra can show up in the physical body as a sore throat or stiffness in the neck or jaw.

The energetic connection between the sacral and throat chakras is undeniable. When the emotional center—the sacral chakra—is stifled, the ability to speak and express these emotions is also altered and muted. This resonates with me because throughout my youth and beyond, I have experienced an intense emotional obstruction, seemingly centered in my throat, which caused me to withdraw and shut down. Feelings of low self-worth and suicidal ideation persisted. I now recognize these as red flag indicators of a clogged root chakra with extreme imbalances. Until efforts are made to unblock these chakras, a person's sense of well-being will remain in distress.

Suffering is inevitable, but it doesn't have to define us—that's the wisdom I found in Buddha's teachings on Dharma and the Four Noble Truths. They provided me a means to hold my pain without being consumed by it. Recognizing that attachment to old narratives and unmet expectations was causing much of my suffering opened the door to genuine relief. For me, practicing Dharma became about living in alignment with truth, compassion, and awareness rather than clinging to control.

Somewhere along the way, I started to grasp what it meant to be present—not just physically but also emotionally and spiritually. Eckhart Tolle's teachings on presence and awakened consciousness helped me recognize how often I was lost in regret about the past or fear about the future. He showed me that peace exists in the now—not in what might happen or what should have happened, but in this breath, this moment. Learning to return to that moment changed everything.

Ralph Waldo Emerson spoke to a part of me that always felt connected to something larger, even when I couldn't name it. His teachings on Transcendentalism invited me to explore that "original relation to the universe" without needing permission or approval. The idea that divinity lives within us—and is accessible through nature, intuition, and solitude—felt freeing and familiar. It reminded me to trust my inner knowing, even when others didn't understand it.

Reading The Divine Comedy became a metaphorical journey for me. Dante's descent into Hell, his slow ascent through Purgatory, and his final arrival in Paradise mirrored my own psychological and spiritual path. There were times when I felt utterly lost in the dark wood, unsure if I would ever emerge. However, the structure of his journey reminded me that transformation is possible—that we are not meant to remain in suffering but to move through it, guided by insight, courage, and love.

And then there's Rumi—the mystic poet whose words felt like a hand on my back in the dark. His poetry didn't just speak to my pain; it walked alongside it. He wrote about fear, loss, longing, and joy, as if they all belonged at the same table. Rumi helped me reframe challenges as invitations rather than punishments. Whenever I felt broken or alone, his words reminded me: "The wound is the place where the light enters you."

Alongside these healing tools, the books I turned

to became companions—wise guides who sat with me in the dark and helped me articulate my feelings. Sometimes they validated my deepest wounds, while other times they challenged me to expand, reframe, or soften. These weren't just books; they were mirrors, maps, and medicine.

Two of the most pivotal works for me as an adoptee were The Primal Wound by Nancy Verrier and Journey of the Adopted Self by Betty Jean Lifton. They gave voice to the ache I had carried all my life—the rupture, the confusion, the quiet, persistent grief of being separated from my first mother. These books didn't try to "fix" adoption or make it palatable. They told the truth, and in doing so, they granted me permission to tell mine.

Then there were works that reminded me of the power of love, not the kind that glosses over pain, but the kind that stays with you through it. "Love Wins" by Rob Bell reminded me that love is stronger than fear and refuses to be weaponized. Brené Brown's "The Power of Vulnerability" reinforced the idea that being open-hearted, even when it's uncomfortable, is the most courageous thing we can do. And in "Bird by Bird" and "Somehow: Thoughts on Love," Anne Lamott reminded me to laugh through the chaos, find God in the mess, and write anyway.

Books like "The Myth of Normal" by Gabor and Daniel Maté and "The Body Keeps the Score" by Bessel van der Kolk, MD, helped me understand the connection between trauma, health, and the body. They reframed my experiences not as character flaws, but as adaptive responses to pain. They offered not just theory, but empathy—and a way forward.

"Breath: The Science of a Lost Art," by James Nestor, explores our most essential biological function and how modern research indicates we may be doing it all wrong. As I learned from my yoga therapist in chapter 7 of this book, "Permission to Breath," being a chest breather and generally breathing incorrectly can severely impact our overall health and sense of well-being.

For structure and philosophy, "The Road Less Traveled" by Scott Peck and "Man's Search for Meaning" by Viktor Frankl grounded me. Peck reminded me that discipline and grace can coexist and that growth often begins with discomfort. Frankl's words—that between stimulus and response there is a space—invited me to pause, breathe, and choose. That idea alone shifted the way I navigate through the world.

Finally, Joseph Campbell's "The Hero's Journey" and Maureen Murdock's "The Heroine's Journey" helped me contextualize my own story. Campbell provided the bones of myth—the descent, the trials, the return—but Murdock spoke to something deeper within me: the return to wholeness through integration, not conquest. Where Campbell's journey ends in triumph, Murdock's continues with healing. I needed both.

These books didn't just inform me; they shaped me. They taught me that healing doesn't mean becoming someone new—it means remembering who you were before the world told you otherwise. What I've shared here—these books, tools, and methods—are pieces of the path that helped me find my way home to myself. They didn't fix me; they didn't erase the past. But they gave me something far more powerful: the capacity to hold my story with tenderness, to witness my pain with less fear, and to trust that healing is possible in layers, over time. These resources reminded me that I wasn't alone, even when I felt most disconnected. And in their own way, each one whispered the same invitation: breathe. Inhale presence, exhale expectation. Inhale truth, exhale shame. Inhale love, exhale fear. My journey isn't about arriving; it's about choosing to breathe, again and again.

14

Satyana

One spring morning, a tall woman in a long, cream-colored robe approached me as I sat quietly beneath the big, old oak tree. She handed me a hand-painted ceramic mandala decorated with geometric patterns and symbols. I took in the beauty of the 8-inch sky-blue turquoise mandala, which had an enticing blend of chocolate brown and navy-blue details.

"My name is Satyana. My name means 'true essence.' I'm the enhanced version of you, dear Emma." She appeared to glide into my view, and with a warm smile, she settled onto the rope-and-wood bench swing.

"You understand and see me clearly when you experience the joy and happiness that come from your desire to value truth above all else, even at the risk of losing something you love."

I immediately recognized her, and my skin began

to glimmer with mystery, integrity, peace, joy, and expansion.

I addressed Satyana slowly: "Some of my other parts, Athena and Justice, say they weren't adopted. I'm curious: Were you? My guess is no."

"You unearthed me, Emma. You didn't always have the choice to do so. I'm here now, helping you integrate all the parts due to the diligent work you've done, especially in the last eight years since you chose to start *fully breathing*. Think of me as Emma 2.0!" Satyana turned her gaze to the sun dipping behind the clouds, casting various shades of color throughout the fading navy blue sky.

She turned back, fixing her gaze on me. "No, I wasn't. Your parents didn't adopt me, nor did I want them to. It was a matter of survival. Knowing that they would intend to annihilate me, my only hope was to be patient and wait for *you to choose me.* I helped you when I could, just like when Athena, your hidden aspect of curiosity, revealed the tool of dissociation during the extreme trauma you and Tim endured at your family's dark wood table in the kitchen every night. When it became safer, I began to instill a yearning for deeper meanings in you."

"How did you do that?" I felt my heart swell.

"Just look out there," she said, sweeping her hand through the air and pointing at the sunset. "How does that make you feel?"

"A sense of awe. Connection. Possibilities. The shades of color make me want to cry; they're so gorgeous," I said, smiling.

"Exactly," Satyana said, giving me a slow, single nod of confirmation. "I also supported your heroic efforts to leave no stone unturned in the search for your birth parents. I planted a seed within you that grew into a force you couldn't ignore or explain. Even when it was time to write your story, I provided you a way to express your integrity—something stifled in you all your life for survival. Using the pseudonym Emma Stevens instead of your real name, Linda Pevac, gave you a voice while protecting your family. And when you were ready, I created the tension within you, guiding you to understand it was time to merge your two names. I laid the foundation that helped you awaken to the need to proclaim your truth, even at the expense of losing everything."

I absorbed Satyana's words, aware of their truth. I have especially felt her guidance over the past eight years. These years are significant because they mark when most things finally began to make sense, at least in a way that allowed me to unravel and examine them honestly.

One of the most remarkable truths I came to understand is that the essence of who I am, or am not, has absolutely nothing to do with the reasons I was relinquished and adopted. My being relinquished and adopted *was not personal!*

Accepting and embracing this as truth, I chose to love myself. Once I accepted that I am lovable and have worth, a flood of other things began to fall into place. I no longer need to make myself small to make others feel more comfortable. I won't stifle my breath just because others say it would be selfish or bothersome for me to take the time for a full inhale and exhale. Admitting that I can set and hold boundaries unapologetically takes practice. Additionally, rewiring my brain to accept these truths has put me on a journey where one truth leads to another and then another.

"When you started seeking me and saying 'yes' to life, even though that often meant sitting with difficult feelings, you stopped blocking your ability to experience creativity and joy. You began to recognize the universe's presence in everything, especially within yourself, dear Emma. Once you began to feel 'real,' *everything* changed for you! You now seek these revelations and are sinking your roots deeper and broader like this big, old oak tree," Satyana said as she gently placed her hand on the tree's bark.

"What makes you feel alive, Emma?" Satyana asked.

"Lots of things. I love it when reciprocity happens in one of my relationships. I get excited by feeling that energetic flow between me and another. Or when I'm outside watching things grow. I feel that enthralling energy then, too. Being creative is also when I feel the most alive. It lights me up inside!" I paused and allowed my thoughts to scan my life for times when I felt real.

"And when you were younger? What things did you do to help you feel this energy?" my wise part asked.

"Unknowingly, I was helping myself feel connected by using my singing voice. There was something so stimulating about feeling my voice vibrate through my body and out of my mouth. One of my most incredible singing experiences was performing a solo at the Senior Assembly of my graduating class, singing 'The Rose' by Bette Midler. The audience gave me a standing ovation, rushed to the front of the stage, helped me down into the crowd, and embraced me," I said, smiling as I recalled.

"Music's narrative role is its ability to tell a story in a way that makes you feel it on a visceral level. Emma, you touched your audience that day! Think of your integration as a climatic musical key change. Each time you identify a new part of yourself, you allow the expansion to create something new, like chord changes that resolve into a new key. It complements the former, but it's gone to a new place."

Satyana's words sent a surge through me. "I'm beyond grateful, Satyana. Thank you for helping me realize that everything is connected and belongs. It's like a paradoxical circle of truth. That means I belong, too."

I looked again at the mandala, still in my hands, marveling at how it symbolizes the universe in its ideal form. Its creation represents the transformation of a universe of suffering into one of joy.

"May I keep this?" I asked.

"Absolutely," Satyana said.

We sat close together and continued to watch the sun as it faded into twilight.

15

Fantasy Shattered

In 1987, I was 23 years old and had been earnestly searching for my birth parents for more than three years. Technically, I had been searching for them my entire life. Each time I looked in the mirror, I wondered who I might resemble. Whenever I saw someone in a crowd, I would ask myself, *"Is that her? Is that my birth mother?"*

I'm not the only adoptee who struggles with these feelings. However, as a same-race U.S. domestic adoptee, I can only imagine the grief and confusion that transracial and intercountry adoptees experience as they have more layers to navigate and understand. Or, a late discovery adoptee who must deal with lies and betrayal from their parents.

After discovering that my birth mother had used a fictitious name throughout her pregnancy but had written a letter signed with her real name to the adoption agency where I was born, I realized that the only way to find her was to obtain that letter. I could only do that by stealing it—so I did. I stole my entire adoption file, including the letter signed by my mother, my original birth certificate, and the notes from the caseworkers who cared for both me and my mother before and after my birth.

Once I had that letter, I was able to find and meet my birth mother shortly afterward. Meeting my birth mother both fortified and devastated me. She was not the mother I imagined in my ghost kingdom. Psychologist, author, and adoptee activist Betty Jean Lifton coined the term "ghost kingdom" to refer to the hypothetical world adoptees enter when imagining their birth relatives. I thought my mother would be more like Samantha Stephens from the hit 1960s television show, *Bewitched*. I was disappointed that she hadn't been relentlessly searching for *me* for the past 24 years, as I had assumed she would be.

While this meeting was invaluable, my idealized image and fantasy of who she was shattered. The woman I encountered disappointed me for many reasons. Primarily, she couldn't provide what I had been searching for all my life: a loving, nurturing mother. She exemplified someone whose "parts of self" were frozen in time. Because she never confronted the trauma of carrying her pregnancy to term, only to relinquish me after nine days, she was the unhealthiest version of herself possible.

As heartbreaking as it was to discover who my first mother was, I would never have realized the other benefits of conducting this search without my pursuit. Over time, I realized that the search had always been more about finding myself than finding her. Nevertheless, I had to search regardless of who my first family was.

What I didn't know then, but I do now, is that the atmosphere and culture of the 1960s, when my mother was expecting me, were not supportive of young, unwed pregnant women. My mother left her home on a farm in Nebraska, where she was the seventh of eight siblings, to live in Denver, where she supported herself as a secretary. That's when she met my father, a cigarette salesman. He was also from a large family and was the youngest of six siblings. They dated and seriously discussed marriage until the day she told him she was pregnant. Even though he was more than 10 years her senior, he ended their relationship, telling her to manage the pregnancy on her own.

Like many young women in the 1960s, she lived in a maternity home for unwed mothers, working odd jobs in exchange for a room and medical care. She never confided to anyone in her entire family of 10 about her pregnancy. She later shared with me how prison-like it felt because of the treatment she and the other pregnant women received from the management and staff. She internalized the shame imposed by society and the maternity home, which led her to believe that she would be selfish to keep her baby, just like so many unwed mothers of that time, and sadly, even today.

In the end, she agreed with the maternity home, the hospital, and society by signing the relinquishment papers, setting in motion both her trauma and mine.

The absence of a loving mother, coupled with meeting my birth mother, who shattered my decades of vivid fantasies about who she would be, made me a target for someone capable of recognizing this trauma within me and exploiting it.

~

As I traveled through the portal to The Gathering Place, I found myself on the rope-and-wood bench swing attached to the big, old oak tree. Its leaves shimmered in vibrant red, green, orange, and yellow shades. I sat still, feeling the gentle autumn breeze and warm sun caress my skin.

My purpose was to meet someone from my past at The Gathering Place, a person who was supposed to have cared for me; however, instead, they took my insides and tried to strangle me with them. This individual from my past had harmed me far more than anyone else I've ever known.

I asked Tabitha to join me in this endeavor since she was the key to understanding how this evil had possessed and colored my life.

We planned to meet in the meadow by the winding stream with its crystal-clear waters and vibrant river rocks. We had come to cherish our time together, sharing our perspectives. Tabitha increasingly embraced her new role as a happy child, unburdened by things that were not hers to carry. She was more than willing to let me handle the more challenging aspects of life.

I held Tabitha's tiny hand as we approached the stream's edge. She squeezed mine, exclaiming, "Can I put my feet in the stream? Please!" She jumped up and down, tugging on my arm.

Nodding, I allowed her to walk along the watery edges of the stream, being careful not to let her slip on the rocks. We followed the winding stream to its deepest point, where tall reeds surrounded the bank. Out of the corner of my eye, I caught a glimpse of something in the water that looked sizable and almost human in shape. Tabitha noticed it, too, as she pulled me closer to get a better look.

"Emma, look! Why is that woman floating on her back in the water?" Tabitha and I were frozen by what we saw.

A mysterious woman was atop the water, adorned in a long, flowing, jeweled, gold-sequined gown with colorful flowers scattered around her. Her flushed cheeks, partially open eyes, and mahogany brown hair drifting in the stream were hauntingly beautiful. Tabitha edged closer, pulling me along as she knelt beside the woman.

"You're so pretty! Lady, are you OK?" Tabitha and I were startled when the woman's gaze focused on us.

An icy chill ran through me as the stunning woman's melodic voice said, *"Tabitha, do you recognize me, darling?"*

The entire scene was ineffable—something straight from Sir John Everett Millais's painting *Ophelia*. What was a character from Shakespeare's *Hamlet* doing here, floating in the stream at The Gathering Place?!

The songbirds sang melodiously, and the sun shone brightly. The sun's rays illuminated the magnificent woman's jeweled, gold-sequined gown, making her appearance surreal.

The woman's face became soft as she continued floating, and her eyes looked lovingly at Tabitha. *"Hold my hand, dear one. I've looked for you for so long. My love for you has never faded. I'm the loving mother you never had but have always yearned for."*

"*Mama!* Where have you been? *I've missed you so much!"* Tabitha exclaimed through a rush of emotion and a flood of tears.

Dropping my hand, Tabitha took the alluring woman's outstretched hand in both of hers.

"Do you trust me, Sweetie?" the woman said lovingly. *"You've always been in my thoughts. Just look at your lovely, glowing skin! So exquisite!"*

Initially, I was captivated by the enchanting woman's charisma and how she seemed to radiate love and goodness. Her beauty alone was mesmerizing, enveloping me with the love I had always longed for. I had always envisioned my first mother would be this: one who would cradle me in her arms and help me grow into something as lovely as she. She would be a strong yet selfless mother who would nurture a secure attachment and be aligned and attuned with me. Tabitha and I were enthralled by the captivating invitation of the woman floating in the stream, declaring her love.

"Baby Girl, float with me. I'll give you all the love you've always wanted. When you feel weak, I'll be your mentor, confidant,

and strength; I'll be your heart's desire!"

The woman was gradually drawing Tabitha into the stream to be beside her. Tabitha briefly slipped on the green, mossy bank but regained her balance by reaching for my arm. A sharp alarm jolted me to my core, warning that things were not as they seemed.

"Tabitha, please step back, sweetheart!" I gently tried to pull her away from the water's edge, keeping my voice soft to avoid scaring her.

Tabitha hesitated but strongly desired to join the mesmerizing woman floating in the water. She inched forward to submerge one of her legs, surrounded by the flowers on the surface.

"No, Tabitha! I think it's a trick! Please listen to me. I believe I know who this woman is. Do *not* trust her!" Panic surged through me as I began questioning who this mysterious woman truly was. I quickly sobered, hoping to caution Tabitha not to go any closer.

"But she's my mama! I've missed her so much. I just want to be with her. Please!" Tabitha's eyes brimmed with tears, revealing the depth of deprivation she had endured throughout her life.

I recognized this dark cloud of deprivation that had once compelled me to embrace fantasies devoid of substance. While they appeared shiny and golden on the outside, they were merely a mirage—sheer deception. Lies that others would use to sap the innate goodness of life from me consumed me until nothing remained, just like fire consumes a forest.

"Don't listen to Emma, darling! I'm here to be your mother."

The bewitching, floating woman's eyes narrowed and flickered red briefly. I shuddered.

"What do you mean? Why wouldn't I listen to Emma?" Tabitha's voice rose an octave. "She's my friend. She's the one who invited me here to The Gathering Place!" Slowly backing away, Tabitha grew suspicious of the woman who claimed to be her loving mother but also seemed to be excluding me.

Suddenly, I recalled a harrowing experience with a woman who had first been my neighbor and then became my psychologist before I realized, almost too late, that she was a sociopath.

"Tabitha, I know who this floating woman is now! She's a psychologist named Dr. Carol Brenner, whom I reached out to for help, but she ended up causing incredible harm to me—us. She had a hidden agenda to make us hers, to move us into her home, and to isolate us from everything and everyone we knew. This is one of those times when you need to trust me to handle the situation. I know you want your needs met, and I intend to address them, but please let me take charge for now," I said imploringly.

Tabitha sobbed as she slowly pulled her leg out of the water and gripped my arm tightly.

The once appealing floating woman suddenly transformed into a vision of darkness. Her withered hand and bony fingers seized Tabitha's ankle with tremendous force, yanking her back into the water.

Tabitha screamed, "Emma! Save me!"

"Come to me, you silly girl! You belong to me! I must have

your youthful beauty!" she spat. The now hideous monster hovered in the water, surrounded by black and brown decaying flowers.

"You can never escape me—I must have you," hissed the monster, Dr. Brenner.

This so-called doctor had managed somehow to unplug my intuition and had groomed me into seeing her as the mother I never had. It was as if she had sedated me into becoming dependent on her and believing everything she said. One horrifying day, she moved all my belongings into her home next door and declared that I was to divorce my husband and consider her my partner instead. I had become so reliant on her that I did whatever she directed—until a glimmer of clarity finally became visible. The professional woman who had claimed to want to be the loving mother I never had morphed into a terrifying monster.

With a firm grip on Tabitha, I shouted to the monster, "Let her go! She *never* belonged to you. You were never the loving mother she needed. You exploited her Achilles' heel and indoctrinated her—a child—with your sick, twisted agenda. IT STOPS NOW. Remove your hands from her and never come here again!"

Once Tabitha was safely back in my arms and we had moved away from the edge of the stream's deep waters, we looked back at the spot where the woman in the flowing, jeweled, sequined gown adorned with colorful flowers had once floated. All that was left were the dead flowers drifting away in the calm, clear waters. The beautiful woman and the hideous monster had both vanished from The Gathering Place.

I focused on Tabitha, saying, "We no longer need to search for a mythical mother to comfort us. The Holy Mystery has called us to become our own mother. I'm the one you seek, little one. I will be the loving mother and parent we never had. I am our source of safety, nourishment, and love. I bring us true peace in wholeness and healing from the wounds of violence. I offer justice and compassion as the essential presence we need to dream and create a new future together. Please let me be that for you."

16

I Am Alive

It's New Year's Eve, and many of us are eager to say goodbye to the current year while looking forward to the next. We always express the same feelings about the year we're leaving behind: "I can't wait for it to end" or "It has been the worst—good riddance." Was the past year truly all bad? Have any previous years been the worst? Or were we simply focused on the negative situations that help shape our narratives? What if these stories aren't true, yet we keep reinforcing them as if they are, creating a self-fulfilling prophecy? Perception and awareness mean everything. Moreover, having contrast in our lives enables us to recognize the ineffable moments, the good enough times, and all the shades of gray that also matter.

In the past year, I have watched over and overseen the construction of my new home—from pouring the concrete to framing, putting on the roof, hanging the front door, and designing a backyard reminiscent of The

Gathering Place—while also figuratively building a new dwelling and a strong foundation within myself. Taking down walls to make room for new, more adaptable ones has been just as demanding and challenging as establishing the healthy boundaries I must uphold unapologetically. My unconscious beliefs made breaking free from the old narrative that much more difficult.

However, I've committed to practicing radical acceptance, resilience, and truth. I strive to use this lens every day. When I revert to familiar old patterns, I extend grace to myself, seek support, and self-correct.

Many of my younger parts, who didn't receive what they needed, emerged while building this new home. I hired what I thought to be a friendly and engaging builder, and we started making plans and determining the budget. However, as the project went on, I began to have questions about overages and invoices and wanted to talk to him about them. He became increasingly difficult to pin down, as he'd assure me, "Yes, next week, for sure! I'll have it all ready to discuss." But then he wouldn't be ready to meet, and instead would assure me everything was fine and offer me a "fist bump." The lack of organization and ability to be transparent continued, with him "bobbing and weaving" whenever I needed to discuss costs. I came to find out, eight months after moving in, that he hadn't paid for some of the lumber for the building of my home, and the vendor placed a lien against my property.

Not only was I furious, but this manipulative behavior reminded me of how I had been ignored, ridiculed, and not taken seriously when I was younger. There was also the perceived fear of deprivation that my newly constructed house would not *feel like home.* That the builder was building me a "broken" house or that I may not have a place to move into at all. Maybe similar to the game of musical chairs, I may find myself with either no chair—or one that may collapse if I sit in it. Allowing my builder to steamroll me into believing he could do whatever he wanted was not something adult Emma could tolerate. Engaging in mediation was the course of action I chose to take with my builder. Although I wasn't fully compensated, I'm proud that I had the courage to stand up to him.

I felt the younger parts of myself silently screaming during the construction of my new home. Justice, Athena, Tabitha, and Mallory surfaced during these challenging times, all seeking acknowledgment yet lacking the voice to express it. Since creating The Gathering Place, I have become more aware of their presence. This experience has given me a unique opportunity to notice them, listen to them, and express gratitude for how I coped in my youth. It has also updated them on how I think, behave, and handle situations today. Emotional regulation was neither modeled nor taught to me in my youth. It was a state of being I had to practice and learn.

While all my parts are welcome, maladaptive behaviors are not. I appreciate these parts, but my adult self decides how to think and behave in the present. Understanding that my younger parts are frozen in time, I am glad to offer them this new, expanded perspective with patience and kindness. I also take the time to practice the essential contemplative art of *pausing* to avoid being reactive in times of stress. As a result, I find myself making better, more informed choices and establishing healthier boundaries.

~

After my parents passed away, I honored their wish for burial in the Golden Cemetery in Colorado alongside my brother. I arranged the transportation of the caskets from Tulsa to Golden. Once they were in their final resting place and the estate sale had concluded, I began to feel the void of their absence. I didn't miss their presence, especially in those last few years, but I must admit they had consumed my entire life in every possible way. If I were to move forward, as most of my instincts urged me to do, I recognized that I needed to grant myself—every part of me—permission to do so.

Over the past year, I've returned several times to the Golden Cemetery to reconcile with the parents who adopted me and the brother I was raised with. My family plot lies at the intersection of Ute and Bison, with cemetery markers identifying where they now rest. I feel a need to check on them to ensure they're still there. I also talk with them, still processing their absence and my childhood, while not fully believing that they no longer exist.

Since I've recreated this same cemetery at The Gathering Place, I can now visit my family without extensive travel. The Golden Cemetery at The Gathering Place resembles the original. Large pink flowering crabapple trees adorn my family's graves, and a snow-capped mountain range is visible in the distance. Visiting also allows me to practice maintaining healthy boundaries even after their passing.

"Hi, Mom and Dad. Hi, Tim," I said softly. "It seems so unfathomable that I'm the last one standing. The one who was deemed least likely to overcome adversity. The one who was told, 'You won't survive without us.'"

I listened as the wind blew through the crabapple tree's branches and leaves. The dirt mounds that once covered my family's graves are now grass. Indicators of the passage of time always strike me as melancholy.

"Emma, how could you let this happen? How could you allow us to die and bury us in the cold earth? This is the most selfish thing you've ever done!" I heard my parents' voices in unison.

Tim added, *"Yeah, I'm supposed to be the smart one. Why do you get to still be alive?"*

My family was expressing thoughts that only my subconscious had considered. I experienced a form of survivor's guilt—an irrational feeling deep within me that just being alive seemed somehow wrong and shameful. My younger self could never have imagined I would outlive my entire family.

"Emma Stevens, get in here with us right now! Stop this ridiculous idea that you deserve to keep living while the rest of us are left behind!" my mother hissed from beyond.

I felt my younger self, Mallory, stirring within me.

The telltale sensation of blame and shame creeping over my flushed face and tightening in my throat and gut gave it away. Mallory felt responsible for others' feelings, behaviors, and decisions. She acted this way to protect me when we were younger.

But instead of letting those feelings overwhelm me and intensify, I paused. In that pause came awareness. In that awareness came choice. I asked Mallory if it would be all right for me to handle this situation that wasn't hers to own. She nodded and took a seat beside me. I asked Justice, Athena, Tabitha, Mallory, and the others the same question, and they all sat beside me, too. They supported me, allowing my adult self to rise to the occasion and utilize the wisdom I had gained to begin reconciling.

Embodying my wisdom, Satyana remained standing with me, guiding my understanding. I closed my eyes and focused on hearing my breath and heartbeat.

Then I heard Satyana whisper, *"Unclench the fists of your spirit and take it easy."* Hearing her words brought me a brief sense of peace.

"No, I don't belong there with you," I retorted to my family's admonishments. "None of you. I know you'd like me to believe that since you always told me I only survived because of you. And Tim, you made choices that shaped your life, and they ultimately caught up with you. You said you never wanted to know your birth parents, but what if there was heart disease in your family history? What if that's why you suffered a fatal heart attack at 60? Wouldn't that have been reason enough to find them? Perhaps that kind of medical information could have motivated you to lead a healthier mental and physical life. You had the right to know!"

As I paused, a realization struck me that if Tim had chosen to use the adoption records I had stolen for him all those years ago to find his birth family, he might still be alive today.

The cloudless sky suddenly darkened. Strong winds whipped my hair across my face, obscuring my vision. I felt an intense energy pulling me toward the graves. Falling to my knees, I rested my hands on the headstone I had designed for my parents.

I whispered, "I will not apologize for being alive. It's not my time yet, and I'll be walking away now. I'll be walking back as someone who has chosen to live authentically. I'm sorry you never chose that for yourselves, even in your last few years. Instead, you chose to try to blame anyone and everyone for your life ending. You will not pull me into your graves!"

I leave with more clarity each time I go to the Golden Cemetery I've recreated at The Gathering Place. I'm grateful for everything; I know it all belongs, even the parts I don't like.

17

Cleo

Satyana and I met on the first day of Autumn, and we planned to walk along the stream in the meadow. I arrived first and was mesmerized by a small jumble of multi-colored river rocks piled at the stream's edge, sending the water cascading over them like a tiny waterfall. The burnt orange and golden yellow leaves and the stones on the bottom of the soft riverbed were reflected in the clear waters. As I stared into the stream, I felt connected to the flow and the mirroring effect. I longed to embody this feeling of happiness, joy, and freedom.

I gazed beyond the red glow of the poison sumac trees to see my wise Self, Satyana, walking the dirt-packed trail towards me. She was not alone—a tall, lean preteen dressed in shorts, a tee-shirt, and athletic shoes who looked like she could run as fast as a cheetah walked beside her. The young girl noticed me first, even though the tall grasses obscured me. In mid-stride, she pivoted to the other side of Satyana but kept her gaze on me. Raising my arm and open hand in the air, I welcomed them to join me by the stream.

Satyana's long, cream-colored dress folded and unfolded around her, mimicking the rippling current of the waters. Her essence and presence were always calming and reassuring.

"Hello, dear Emma!" Satyana said, embracing me. "I've brought someone with me today. Her name is Cleo, which means 'to celebrate.' Unfortunately, her parents didn't quite live up to that."

The young girl switched sides of Satyana, darting to and fro, never standing still. I also noticed how her appearance would shift constantly: one second looking tall, the following short. Then her eyes, bright green, turned to hazel.

"Cleo is the part of us with a chameleon-like nature, Emma. Her role was to protect you—*at all costs*. I asked her to come today because she has a story to tell, and I knew you'd want to hear it. It will be invaluable. I invite you to listen to her intently. She's key to freeing you to move forward on your labyrinth," Satyana said.

Careful not to make sudden moves, I gave Cleo a welcoming smile and greeting. I was assessing Cleo's apparent chameleonic nature and her hypervigilance. Growing up in an alcoholic home, one learns how to tuck, duck, and roll—it's harder to hit a moving target.

Cleo was proving this point as Satyana and I watched her stealthily maneuver from standing by the stream to hiding in the weeds to sitting on a nearby old tree stump. I empathized with Cleo's intense attentiveness. An idea popped into my mind.

Looking at Satyana and then focusing on Cleo, I said, "What would you think about going up the hill to the big, old oak tree and playing on the swing?" It would not be the first time the swing at The Gathering Place had empowered my parts to tell their stories.

Cleo gave a wary nod, which I took as a yes. We walked the short distance up the hill to the swing. I crafted the questions and thoughts I would share with her. I wanted to go slowly and gently to put her at ease.

"How long has the swing been here?" Cleo questioned.

"Not long, just a few years. Why?" I asked.

"Are you sure it's safe? What if I get on it and it falls?" Cleo seemed fearful and anxious about the integrity of the swing.

"How about I swing on it first, and you can judge for yourself? You don't have to take a turn if you don't want to," I said.

"Hmm … OK." Cleo looked doubtful but stayed with us.

I was encouraged that Cleo might get in the swing. The repetitive swinging movements might calm her, allowing her to tell her story.

Satyana and Cleo watched as I stood before the rope-and-wood bench swing. I walked backward with it a few steps and hopped into the seat, letting the momentum glide me forward in the air and then back. My speed accelerated as the gravitational energy increased. A graceful harmony happens with the oscillation motion of swinging, and the synchronization can result in feeling calm and relaxed. Both swinging and gentle rocking can have this effect. Feeling the wind in my hair made me happy.

Almost forgetting that Satyana and Cleo were watching, I let my thoughts drift to how I often feel joyous now. This metamorphosis happened after I became dedicated to getting to know myself. The result is loving myself and others more authentically.

One of the tools I use is the Enneagram. "The Enneagram is a personality typing system that describes patterns in how people interpret the world and manage their emotions. There are nine Enneagram Personality Types, each of which has its key motivations and fears that largely guide their actions and decisions," according to The Enneagram Institute. I've often heard Typology Podcast host and author Ian Morgan Cron refer to the Enneagram as a tool that "Does not put you in a box. It shows you the box you're already in and how to get out." We all possess elements of all nine types within us, yet we tend to gravitate toward one particular personality type that explains our behaviors and motivations. The concepts help me see the motivation behind my actions and behaviors, both in and out of health. I find it incredibly useful in trying to become the highest expression of myself.

Along my sobriety path (behaviorally and emotionally), I discovered the difference between transformation and reformation. Reformation changes form, but transformation is an internal change that becomes something new. I was fortunate enough to keep digging deeper until I experienced a life-giving transformation. I realized that until I dealt with my core issues of relinquishment, adoption, and the family dysfunction I grew up in, I may temporarily solve one problem, but the underlying issues would only shift into a new problem. *I can't be in bondage and flourish.*

"OK," Cleo said. "I'm ready now. I'm ready to sit in the swing." Cleo stopped biting her fingernails long enough to position herself on the swing. She sat staring at her gym shoes on the grassy ground beneath.

"Are you going to tell my parents I'm here? *Please* don't tell them. I'd get into a lot of trouble. You know, I think I should leave now and get back before anyone notices I'm gone." Cleo stood and looked ready to sprint down the hill.

Satyana stepped forward, saying, "Wait, Cleo! Remember our earlier talk when I explained that your family is gone now? And that you've grown up? Look at Emma. This is the future you! You made it! You no longer need to run from your past, but I know it will take time and patience to accept and understand. Your trauma, dear Cleo, is in your nervous system. Emma and I are working diligently to bring you peace, joy, and happiness."

Cleo looked like a deer in the headlights, unsure whether to bolt or stay and listen.

My eyes sought hers. "Yes, Cleo. Satyana is right. Can you please stay a while and share your story?"

Cleo sat back down, shutting her eyes tight. "What do you mean my parents *are gone?* Wherever they've gone, I guarantee they'll be back! I've been fooled by thoughts that things will be different—only to see that I

CAN NEVER LET MY GUARD DOWN."

Satyana gently placed her hands on Cleo's elevated shoulders and watched as they slowly lowered. She said, "Would it be all right if I give you a soft push to get you started, Cleo?"

I stood beside Cleo as she started pumping her legs to gain momentum. Cleo's firm body control was evident as she moved with little effort.

"So, you want to hear my story? I'll tell you. I have to spend all my time protecting myself. When I don't, or I forget, I pay for it. My parents do not play fair. I try to be on my toes, always try to guess what might happen next, and be ready to change on a dime—depending on their moods at any given time. I don't have time to be a kid! I'm too busy being on high alert to ensure my survival."

"What would you rather be doing, Cleo?" I asked.

"Are you kidding? A million things!" Cleo said as the arc of her swing got higher and higher.

"Like what exactly?" I pressed.

"I wish I didn't have to care for my parents' feelings, for example! I wish they wouldn't hurt me! I wish my face weren't puffy from crying all night and feeling like I had to crawl to school the next day. I wish I could be with my friends and participate in school groups. They make my brother and me live in isolation in the country without kids to play with. Summers are a nightmare alone with my mother. It's like she takes pleasure in telling us, *'You think that hurts? Just wait until your father gets home!'*

I had to learn how to hide from her, to make myself small, and make apologies I never meant. I learned these things to try to keep both of them happy. Why did she even want children?! I wish my parents wouldn't scream and hit each other and then turn it around on Tim and me. They drink every night, and I see my mom's eyes shift and flash anger, and my dad shakes the ice in his Bourbon glass and starts acting like a bully. I wish I didn't have to watch my dad hit and kick my brother to the ground while screaming, *'Be a man, goddammit!'"* Cleo paused to breathe.

"I would rather have a mother and a father who love me—ones who wrap their arms around me and comfort me—a mom who makes me feel whole when I'm sad. A mother who celebrates me instead of being jealous. A father who protects me no matter what. Parents who advocate for me and listen when I tell them that something is wrong. Parents who would tell me where I came from so I don't feel so lost and alone and like I'm from outer space," Cleo said as her swing came slowly to a stop, face wet with tears.

Kneeling before Cleo, I looked up at her and said, "Those were truly awful days." Then, I let silence envelop us. "I hope you'll hear me when I say, *Thank you, Cleo.* Thank you for your hypervigilance that helped keep us 'safer.' Your strategies were clever and, most often, effective. We could not have made it through without you and the others."

Cleo stepped from the swing into my arms. We held each other. Satyana spread her arms around us as we held space for Cleo and her story.

"I have something to show you, Cleo," I said. Satyana nodded; she knew where we were going next.

As we walked into the cemetery at The Gathering Place, I paused in front of my parents' graves, where they shared a headstone. The massive pink flowering crabapple was always in bloom at my gathering place.

"Cleo, I've brought you here to see that our parents have passed. I know that, in your awareness, it seems as though that's not true. Satyana and I will be with you to help you begin to understand this. We want to give you rest. You've been keeping guard for a lifetime. It's time for you to let me do the heavy lifting," I said.

"Emma is right, Cleo. When we are fearful and anxious, it keeps us from the highest expression of ourselves. It keeps us from our creativity, which blocks our ability to experience beauty, awe, and wonder. Emma has discovered that when she experiences her creativity, it puts her in a continuous loop of having a sense of well-being. A state of being she now holds dear," Satyana said.

"Your remarkable ability to hyperfocus could evolve into a healthier role in safeguarding our energy and helping us say 'yes' to life. And you won't be alone this time, Cleo! I'll be there to guide and comfort you," I said, feeling reassured by my words.

"I've never asked myself what *I* want. My concern has always been about what others want me to do and think," Cleo said, eyebrows raised.

"What if you didn't have to do that anymore?" I said.

Cleo's expression looked softer. I saw hope in her eyes.

Hypervigilance was still active—but changing.

18

Disequilibration

I recently came across a word that holds special meaning for me: *disequilibration*. It means to place out of balance. The first time I think I experienced this was in utero. From the notes I took from the adoption agency where I was adopted, I learned that my birth mother attempted to self-terminate her pregnancy at seven months. I certainly felt the trauma, along with sensing and reacting to emotions such as love and rejection, as well as more complex feelings like ambivalence and ambiguity. A mother's thoughts about her child and/or pregnancy—love, rejection, or disinterest—can directly affect the child's subsequent sense of self, security, and self-esteem.

A disequilibration most definitely happened when my birth mother relinquished me, separating me from everything I'd ever known, followed by spending the first three formative months of my life in a foster house with other babies awaiting adoptive families. All the while, I patiently waited while feeling the deprivation of missing my mother.

Next on my timeline was meeting more strangers, but these strangers were now to become my parents. I also met my brother, Tim, the only other adoptee in my life.

Disequilibration struck my life again when, at 18 months, I decided to stop eating and drinking liquids. I was hospitalized for severe dehydration and received intravenous feeding until I stabilized. The two access points on each of my outer thighs, about the size of a quarter, remain visible all these decades later. I genuinely believe this happened because I felt a profound emptiness and deprivation, as my birth mother never returned, and I lacked genuine care from the mother who was raising me.

Navigating life's dissonance became my norm and shaped my understanding of how I should move through the world. The nuanced impacts of adoption on the mind, body, and nervous system are now being studied. Adoption, as currently defined, is most often a failed social experiment despite the persistent view that adoption is beautiful. Even without the abuses inflicted by my adoptive parents, the trauma of relinquishment and adoption alone affected my healthy physiological development.

The disequilibration that happened to me at eleven years old was intensely painful. I was devastated when I learned I'd be moving with my family to Tulsa. I had to leave my school, friends, and the neighborhood pool in Oklahoma City, which I'd regularly visit in the summertime. Change and goodbyes are particularly difficult for adoptees. For me, it mimicked my first experience in life: abandonment and loss.

Further disequilibration occurred after the move when my parents allowed my new school to place me in a class for academic underachievers, claiming it was the only class with space for me. I was affected by this, but even more by my parents' inaction in correcting the situation.

My world felt impossible to navigate when the new house my parents built was in a rural area, isolated from neighbors and children my age. It was an hour-and-a-half bus ride to school each way.

Even more destabilizing was that my brother and I felt held captive by our mother, who needed to make us suffer for her inadequacies. The oppression was worse during the summers when we didn't have school as an escape. Life felt grim, like a constant walk on eggshells.

Chaos and sudden emotional outbursts were a regular occurrence in our alcoholic family. My mother's drinking intensified her resentment towards my brother and me, perceiving us as burdens in her life. She would fill my father's mind with tales of how we had misbehaved that day and demand he punish us when he got home.

To make matters worse, he often returned home late at night after taking clients out for drinks. He would stumble in late and be intoxicated. My mother would hold dinner for him, forcing my brother and me to sit at the hardwood dinner table with empty plates before us until his arrival. As soon as my father walked through the door, our parents would immediately engage in a terrible drunken fight, using words designed to insult and hurt. Dinner might or might not happen after that. Ultimately, their anger would turn on my brother and me, leaving us in tears.

The night would end with them saying, "But remember, we love you! And we don't even see you as adopted." While this may seem like an innocuous thing to say, to an adopted person, it's a denial of their reality. These types of statements, called microaggressions, send the message to adoptees that they had no past before their adoption and that they should be grateful for their adoptive parents accepting them as their own. Another example of a microaggression is telling an adopted person, "Your first mom loved you so much, she placed you for adoption." I know this phrase deeply troubled and confused me regarding what love meant. Did being loved by someone equal abandonment?

After graduating from college, I moved to California to begin work at an advertising agency. By then, I had discovered my birth mother and connected with my future husband. These new people in my life brought imbalance, as well. My birth mother shattered all my fantasies about who I thought she would be and what I believed meeting her would mean to me. The man I thought I loved and married turned out to be much like my adoptive mother: punitive, jealous, and narcissistic.

All of this led to the most profoundly negative disorientation I've ever experienced—and ultimately to being indoctrinated and exploited by a psychologist I hired to help me with my past unhealthy experiences. Instead, I found myself dealing with a sociopathic psychologist who had a dangerously negligent personal agenda aimed at possessing and controlling me. This ordeal was one I nearly didn't survive, as little support was available to deprogram me following the cultic one-on-one relationship.

A little more than eight years ago, an immensely *positive* upheaval occurred. The turning point came when I recognized that my unhealthy relationship with alcohol needed to end; if it didn't, it would end me. The benefit of reaching the end of yourself is that one of your only options is to ask for help. I found the willingness to remain willing and let the Holy Mystery instill in me the courage to accept that I could not achieve this alone. I got sober, which was no small feat!

When I attended a Twelve-Step Program, I learned it was only *one* aspect of my life that needed cleaning up. I felt overwhelmed. It had taken all my strength just to get sober. I even had to navigate a slight relapse. But I persevered. I continued attending Twelve-Step meetings, researching, and growing. I practiced yoga and meditation. I began writing and singing again and noticed my relationships improved. I started practicing emotional sobriety and learning its true meaning. Finding an ethical and empathic counselor was paramount. The expansion I began to feel was indescribable. These discoveries became the fuel that propelled me forward, even though it forced me to confront my immense grief and trauma. My new counselor told me, "Emma, you can more easily change your beliefs about not being 'enough' because your willingness to grow and expand is much stronger!"

All my unresolved grief and trauma began to emerge and collide, demanding my attention. It's incredible how much you can accomplish when you get sober and your brain heals! As a result, I experienced a heightened awareness of numerous issues. I started questioning everything I had ever known, everything I believed, and how my family and society had conditioned me.

As an adoptee, I have become increasingly aware of how my entire life has been shaped and molded by relinquishment and adoption. Not one decision I've ever made or thought about myself has been free from the perspective of being an adopted person. I had been conditioned to believe in a false narrative about myself, and it was up to me to dismantle and deconstruct that narrative and discover a new way of being in the world. The journey is fraught with obstacles, including losing people whom I believed were my friends because they don't appreciate the new healthy boundaries I set. It's difficult. It's sometimes sad. Yet, choosing authenticity over conforming to the status quo is rewarding.

I've learned that disequilibration doesn't have to be unfavorable; instead, it often serves as the necessary tension that leads to transformation. Vietnamese monk and peace activist Thích Nhất Hạnh discusses the importance of holding our anger with love. When managed in a healthy and loving manner, anger can transform into something more—something that nurtures life. In the liminal space where I'm growing and changing, I remember to pause and notice how the intersectionality of everything is evident when I choose to look.

19

The Gift of Anger

I have unresolved anger that feels red-hot within me. I'm hesitant to admit out loud that I feel this anger, but since I've never known how to direct it, I'm choosing to express it on paper. Writing is therapeutic, and I believe that expressing anger requires both space and care.

If I were to give the part of me that identifies as anger a name, it would be *Smoke*. Just as with other parts of myself, I've invited her to meet me at The Gathering Place. She is reluctant to come bearing the identity of anger, as many women would be because we're taught from an early age that anger is not an appropriate emotion for a female. However, like all my other parts, Smoke is always welcome on these green, grassy hills.

In the invitation to Smoke, I indicated that this meeting should occur at her convenience. There was no hurry. I expressed my desire to hear from and see her. I did not judge or expect anything. I was open to letting this meeting unfold naturally without my interference.

If anger signals when something is wrong, much was amiss in my brother and my adoptive home. My mother would mention how my brother Tim held his breath to the point of nearly passing out as a toddler. She would laugh about how bright red his cheeks became instead of learning how to be a mother to him. Tim was using the only way he could to communicate and meet his needs before using words. My brother needed her to help him regulate his emotions, but she, in turn, taught him that his feelings were amusing to her.

I managed my anger toward her in much the same way: I suppressed it. I internalized it and convinced myself that it was necessary for my survival, telling myself it was the best way to eliminate my anger. However, just like Tim holding his breath, we both risked imploding from our unexpressed anger.

With my eyes closed and my mind open, I imagined a part of myself named Smoke and wondered what she looked like: a figure dressed in varying shades of gray, with black scarves billowing in the wind. Her hands were adorned with slim-fitting crimson gloves, and she gripped a walking stick. Smoke's long, curly black hair seemed wild, reminiscent of the snake-haired Medusa.

A loud clap of thunder opened my eyes wide, and I saw The Gathering Place engulfed in a snow and lightning storm known as a thundersnow. This was highly unusual. The Gathering Place's skies were often bright and filled with lovely, wispy clouds. Could my guest, Smoke, have arrived? She stood in the tall grasses, her scarves and hair whipping in the wind, lightly dusted with snow.

We moved closer, narrowing the gap between us. A wave of anxiety washed over me as I realized I had denied and ignored Smoke for much of my life. What if she lashed out at me? She had a right to do that. She had been suppressing her anger for so long. I was instantly strengthened by remembering my wise self, Satyana, who says, *"We can do hard things."* The path to integrity involves placing truth above my need for the comfort of remaining in the status quo.

"Are you Smoke? Are you the part of me that holds my anger?" She looked at me, and for a long moment, I thought she might not answer.

"That's me. I held our anger and attempted to metabolize and digest the vast amounts." Smoke took her red-gloved hand and tried smoothing down her hair, but the blustery wind persisted.

She continued, "I am weary. Why have you asked me to come?"

"Smoke, I've come to share a few significant things with you." I shivered from the cold and crossed my arms to warm myself.

"First, I want to thank you. I'm truly sorry it was such a difficult and heavy load. You helped us persevere and navigate those times that felt impossible. All those moments you felt smothered by your anger without a place to let it go."

Another loud clap of thunder and a flash of lightning

jolted me. In that brief moment of light, Smoke seemed younger than when I first saw her in the distance. Also noticeable was a smoldering, flameless mist radiating off her body, even though the temperature was below freezing.

"I tried my best to contain the anger and injustices so you could focus on gathering all the resilience and courage you could," Smoke confessed.

"Well, it worked! The younger parts you're referring to are Mallory and Tabitha. They persevered because of your valiant efforts. I've been having meaningful conversations with them to update them on how much things have changed in our lives."

"Update them on what?" Smoke tilted her head, her wild hair whirling in the wind.

"That's another reason I asked you to meet me here at The Gathering Place. I apologize for taking so long to tell you that today differs from the past because now I have choices. You had to suppress all our anger back then, but we've grown up and are on a different path."

The next thunderous lightning bolt jolted me as it struck dangerously close. My hypervigilance has led to an overdeveloped startle response, particularly to sudden, loud noises. The continuous abuse I received as a child resulted in complex post-traumatic stress.

"Smoke, is it *you* causing the thunder, snow, and lightning?" I jumped from where I stood as if I could find a safer spot.

"And what's your plan for me to rid myself of all the unresolved grief that has turned into anger, despair, and hate?"

Smoke threw down the walking stick and raised her red-gloved hands toward the snowy sky in protest.

I felt the ground rumble beneath my feet as I tried to fill my lungs with a deep, cleansing breath.

"I'm listening, Smoke. Go ahead," I said.

"You can't even remember most of what happened! I helped you block it out because you wouldn't have been able to handle it. *You have no idea!*" Smoke exclaimed as she unleashed another jarring bolt of lightning.

She leaned her head back and let out a long, soulful, even-toned cry that resonated like the tears of everything. Simultaneously, a grayish-black vapor escaped from her mouth. I felt like I was witnessing something holy and transformative. Smoke's piercing voice rang throughout the hills and meadow of The Gathering Place as if to reclaim the dignity, honor, and grace stolen from her by her parents and others.

I sat in the snow, watching and listening to Smoke. My heart swelled with love as I felt I was witnessing the mystery of who she was.

After a long struggle and emotional outpouring, she settled next to me. Smoke looked exhausted. I also allowed myself to sit with the uncomfortable and painful experiences from decades past. I sensed the weight on my chest. It felt heavy, dark, and oppressive.

She was right that I wouldn't have been able to bear all the anger and pain of my childhood. My solution was often to go into a dissociative state. If I had considered telling anyone I was angry, the outcome would not have been in my favor. For my anger to be deemed legitimate and worthy of being heard, it would first need to have been recognized that I had a right to have needs.

Today, I feel angry about how women are treated in this country and elsewhere. When a man shows his anger, we see him as brave and strong. However, when a woman expresses the same anger, she's viewed as problematic or labeled with derogatory names. It seems unfathomable that women are still fighting for equal rights and are told what they can or cannot do with their lives and their bodies.

Eventually, I realized that the thunder and lightning had ceased. Only large, fluffy snowflakes kept falling. As silence enveloped us, I heard an owl's persistent, melodic hoots calling to another in the trees beyond. It was a comforting sound, easing my sadness.

"Smoke, I have an idea. I'm not saying it will solve everything, but will you let me show you something?" I said hopefully, standing up and brushing off the snow. To my amazement, Smoke stood up as well.

With a smile, I suggested, "It would be much easier to take you there if the sun were shining and we didn't have to worry about being struck by lightning. What do you think?"

I led her to an old red brick ledge that bordered one edge of the lake at The Gathering Place. Some of the bricks were loose and crumbling. Noticing the now-sunny sky, I waved Smoke over to join me on the ledge. I gave her a nod and a smile for the sudden weather change. We sat silently for a while.

"Smoke, one thing that has changed is that I've

learned how to breathe. Do you understand what I mean by that? I used to avoid breathing fully; my hypervigilance held me back. However, my new breathing technique, which involves taking deep belly breaths and fully exhaling, calms my nervous system. It's been incredibly helpful, especially during stressful times and when I feel angry. I try to remind myself not to breathe shallowly."

As I looked at Smoke, I grabbed a loose brick and held it firmly. Lifting it over my head, I hurled it into the nearby lake, watching it make a messy splash.

"*That* was for all the times my parents made my brother and me sit at the kitchen table and listen to them drunkenly berate us!" I said with conviction.

"Now it's your turn!" I handed Smoke a brick.

"OK, I can do this," Smoke said. "This is for all the times they abandoned me, and I had to pretend it didn't bother me!" The brick soared through the air farther than I could throw mine and smashed into the lake.

As she launched another brick into the lake, Smoke declared, *"This one is for those who didn't consider how painful it would be for me to lose my mother and the rest of my birth family on the day I was born!"*

My next brick to throw with all my might was the conditioning and grooming I underwent, which led me to believe a false story about myself—preventing me from knowing myself.

I passed Smoke another brick, then another, and another. She shared with me how she felt exhilarated by the sense of restored power it gave her. We shed many sorrowful and angry tears, lightening our spirits one brick at a time.

Smoke and I now meet regularly at The Gathering Place, where we've found a way to express our anger without harming ourselves or others. Often, things get awkward and messy, and suppressed anger emerges in unexpected ways. However, I promised Smoke I would give her all the space, bricks, and time needed to unload and unburden. I also assured her she was no longer alone in dealing with her unresolved anger. In her own time, she will embrace anger as a healthy emotion when rooted in love and allowed to foster transformation.

20

What's in a Name

What's in a name? Does it define who we truly are? In *Romeo and Juliet*, William Shakespeare suggests it does not. "A rose by any other name would smell as sweet."

My name at birth was Baby Girl Lockridge. This was a fictitious name. It was given to me by my first mom, who had also given herself a fabricated name during her stay at the home for unwed mothers while pregnant with me.

In March 1962, I was adopted by my new parents to play the role of a dutiful, compliant daughter who would address their infertility issues and fulfill their emotional needs. The first three months after my relinquishment at birth in January were spent in a foster home, where many infants awaited legal adoption. Until I was transferred to my adoptive parents, I was only known as Baby Girl Lockridge, and they renamed me Linda Sue Campbell.

Growing up, I never warmed to my middle name. That was my adoptive mom's name. Sue was her middle name, but she most often went by the name "Sue." I didn't identify with the name Linda Sue because it was her name, and she wasn't very kind to me. I wanted to distance myself from anything that seemed to make me feel absorbed by her, especially when she went so far as to say we "looked just alike." While my mom was an attractive woman, it was one more way she messed with my reality by claiming something as true that just wasn't.

Even as a toddler, I felt her need to mold me into her image. It was at that age that I was told I was adopted. My first reaction was to weep for my first mom. I expressed concern and wanted reassurance that she was OK. I asked if she missed me. Much like in the 1937 Disney movie, *Snow White and the Seven Dwarfs*, where the Evil Queen demands, "Magic mirror, on the wall—who is the fairest one of all?" I quickly learned of my mom's deep jealousy toward anything that did not revolve around or glorify her. My care and concern for my first mom were deeply resented, sparking intense red anger within Sue, my mom. Just like the Evil Queen, who would order death to anyone or anything that dared suggest someone could be "more fair than thee," my survival depended on keeping my needs and true self tightly under wraps.

Shortly after I learned it was taboo to speak of my adoption or dare ask about my adoption story, I began fantasizing about my birth mother. Who was she? Did I look like her? Did she think about me—maybe even miss me? I was a child of the 1960s and 1970s, watching *The Brady Bunch*, *The Partridge Family*, *Gilligan's Island*, and *I Dream of Jeannie* on TV. But the show I fixated on was *Bewitched*, featuring Samantha, Tabitha, and Darrin (Dick York, the actor who played the first Darrin!). I imagined beautiful, magical Samantha as my birth mom and envisioned myself as the adorable little Tabitha Stephens. I would daydream about how Samantha could effortlessly mend the hole in my motherless soul with a twitch of her nose, just like magic.

And with that, my fantasy life began. My attention turned to all things shiny, things that were fantastical. However, there were frequent moments when my immediate attention was needed to keep myself out of harm's way due to my parents' emotional outbursts, which often became violent. Living in fantasy, or dissociating, became a preoccupation with desiring people, places, and things that might seem full of promise initially, but upon closer examination, were clearly unhealthy for me.

My chosen profession after college was what I had always fantasized about: the exciting world of advertising. After all, it was good enough for Darrin Stephens from *Bewitched*, wasn't it? It sounded creative, fast-paced, and glamorous—including attending photoshoots. However, it was anything but. It was also where I met the creative director of the agency, who became my husband, resulting in yet another name change as I took his last name. When I went to the Social Security office to make my married last name official, I took the opportunity to eliminate my middle name, Sue, and replace it with my maiden name. I became Linda Campbell Pevac.

Both my husband and my profession shattered any illusions I had about their creativity or beauty. Instead, I discovered deception. The truth was that I had bought into the facade and ignored the wisdom that says, "When something seems too good to be true, it probably is." Damn my tendency for fantasy.

Much later, I found myself on a healing path that living in the present tends to immerse people in. It took relearning, discarding, and reconstructing everything I had ever believed to be true, including redefining my sense of self. While I was ready to finally express the wisdom I had gained about loving what is solid and true—rather than needing to make things deceptively "shiny"—I ironically chose to write under a fictitious name: a pseudonym. I did this for the compassionate reason of wanting to protect my family.

I wrote two books under my pseudonym, and that has served me well. One advantage of using #EmmaStevensWriter to author *The Gathering Place: An Adoptee's Story* and *A Fire Is Coming* is that it's been much easier to write such vulnerable material than it would have been as Linda. Using a pseudonym, or "false name," provided me with a buffer or shield that offers a layer of protection. I do not regret using the pseudonym. The name Emma helped define one of my "parts" within Linda. Getting to know my writer persona, Emma, has actually deepened my self-understanding. I believe it has protected both me and my family.

However, using the assumed name of Emma Stevens—I took creative license with the spelling of the last name of the Stephens family in *Bewitched*—has messed with my psyche again by attributing my books, social media presence, and guest episodes on numerous podcasts to Emma. This often led to confusion, not only for me but also for the podcast hosts, as I would ask them to call me Emma during recording. I have had to maintain a clear distinction across multiple social media accounts, ensure my picture isn't posted as Emma, and be cautious about being "tagged" in posts, which may compromise my anonymity.

Using a pseudonym began to evoke a sense of secrecy and deception. One insight I've gained from my experiences as an adoptee and as someone in recovery from unhealthy patterns is that "our secrets only make us sick." I realized I wanted to be more *like Emma* than being my true self. The ongoing reliance on fantasy in my life raised a red flag for me. I started to feel curious about the changes occurring in my sense of identity.

Now that my last parent has recently passed away, I feel a strong inclination for Linda Campbell Pevac to absorb Emma Stevens as a vital, creative, and beautiful part of myself. However, Linda is my core. I have many facets, just as we all do, and all those parts are welcome. I'm now at a point where becoming whole and starting on the path of integration is imperative. I've also discovered that I am Linda, regardless of whichever name I choose to go by. Thus, my answer to the question, "Do our names define us?" is both yes and no. Above all, I believe we define ourselves.

Emma Stevens will write again. When I do, I will choose to use that name to continue fostering my brand recognition. However, my identity is Linda. The two will be inextricably linked in the healthiest, life-giving ways as we move forward.

To all who have helped me maintain my mask as Emma, please know how much I appreciate you. Thank you for the love and support you've shown me. I'm grateful and humbled by the grace and respect you've given. Both Linda and Emma will never forget it.

21

A Final Goodbye

My former husband, Rick, died today.

He died as a result of many things: physical, mental, and spiritual. His death certificate will likely list the cause of death as cardiac arrest, cessation of blood circulation, and breathing. Similar to my brother, who suffered his first heart attack at 58, Rick also suffered a stroke a few years ago. Doctors advised my brother and Rick to change their lifestyles, but neither of them listened.

Rick did not like doctors and would wait until he was in excruciating pain to seek medical attention. A few weeks ago, Rick was hospitalized with an infected toe. While he had told others it was nothing serious, the doctor diagnosed it as gangrene. At first, my kids and I learned he might have to consider amputation, but soon, his extremely low blood pressure, decreased oxygen levels, and lack of blood flow became insurmountable.

His health condition became an all-systems failure.

I divorced Rick in 2006. We were married for 12 years and had two exceptional children together. Dana and Trevor were, and remain, the essence of my life. When the children were young and needed all my attention, I was able to distract myself from feeling miserable about Rick's lack of moral character—someone who considered himself exempt from paying taxes to the Internal Revenue Service, had his paycheck garnished for unpaid back child support, borrowed large sums of money from my parents and friends without any intention of repaying them, and whose sense of entitlement overshadowed every aspect of his life. No relationship in his life was unscathed by his narcissism.

While I haven't seen Rick in over eight years, my adult children often talk about his words or deeds. They struggle with his life choices, namely ignoring his health issues that were contributing to a slow decline. I try to remain neutral, but I frequently fail. Regardless, Dana and Trevor have decided on their opinions and the amount of contact they want with their dad. During Rick's recent hospitalization, it was difficult for my children to understand their father's procrastination in seeking medical treatment, which ultimately led to his death. He lived in a similar way to how he died—without genuine respect and love for others or even for himself.

Rick and I met when I was 24. I had just moved to Southern California and had begun working at an advertising agency. Rick, 20 years my senior, was an associate creative director at the same agency. I found him charming and good-looking. He showered me with attention, and I attached to him immediately.

As Rick and I became more serious, I remember telling myself that age was just a number and all that mattered was that we loved each other. My emotional maturity and stability were precarious, and I felt I needed Rick to survive. I came into the relationship with a plethora of unresolved traumas and unhealthy conditioning instilled by my family. I placed all my trust in Rick to save me from the oppression and manipulation I had endured since being relinquished by my first mother and then adopted by my parents. Rick portrayed himself as a sort of guru on an enlightened path. I wanted him to make me whole. Years later, I realized Rick was full of empty promises. His narcissism prevented him from showing up for anyone but himself.

~

Today was the day. Rick convinced me there was no other choice. I was going to have the procedure, and that was final. I agonized over the decision but ultimately chose to trust Rick. I was angry with him, though I was angrier with myself for not being more careful.

The nurse inserted the intravenous drip into my hand. That was the last thing I remember feeling: the burning sensation of the anesthesia flowing into my bloodstream as I tried to count backward from 10. "Nine … eight … seven …" and then I was out.

When I began to regain consciousness, I heard

muffled voices and the sounds of people moving in the room. I felt a touch on my hand followed by a gentle adjustment of my arm. A voice that seemed distant called my name.

"Emma, it's time to wake up now. Can you hear me? It's time to wake up." I felt a gentle shake of my arm again. "We can't release you until you have someone to drive you home," the nurse said to me in the recovery room at the outpatient clinic.

I was still groggy, but I muttered, "He said he'd be here. I'm sure he's outside waiting."

Remembering where I was and why I lay on a hospital bed at this clinic made me slam my eyes shut again, feeling hot tears. I fell asleep.

"Let's sit you up and have some sips of water. It's not good to take in too much after having anesthesia. I'm going to raise the bed for you now, all right? My name is Nurse Bobbie."

Awake again, I had to admit that a drink of water sounded appealing for soothing my throat. I was uncertain why it was so sore, but I didn't want to ask to find out. At 24, I wasn't confident enough to ask too many questions.

The nurse continued explaining the post-surgery instructions. "You'll need bed rest for the next few days, and you should call this number if you experience any pain. Moderate cramps are normal, though."

After the water, Nurse Bobbie helped me get dressed. I brought the loose clothing that the clinic recommended I wear home. I signed all the paperwork necessary for my release and was eager to leave the clinic. I wanted to distance myself as much as possible from the experience I had just chosen to endure.

"I'll take you to a phone where you can call to find out where your ride home is," she said as she guided me to the wheelchair and wheeled me to the front of the building.

"Uh, OK," I said. "I'm sure my boyfriend is on his way." However, I wasn't entirely confident that Rick was coming. We had only lived together briefly, which left me feeling insecure and uncertain about who Rick actually was. I was even more unsure of who I was. I dialed the number of the advertising agency where Rick and I both worked.

"Good afternoon, Foote Cone & Belding. How may I direct your call?"

I struggled to find my voice through my sore throat, saying, "Rick Dorsey, please."

When the receptionist returned to the line, she announced, "Rick is in the conference room for a client meeting. I'm not sure how long he'll be busy. May I take a message?"

My face flushed hot and red. Rick knew my procedure was today and when he would need to pick me up. I had driven to the clinic, but Rick decided I would leave my car there, and we would go home in his.

He was *not* on his way.

Looking down, I covered my face with one hand to hide my tears. After leaving a message saying Rick needed to pick me up as quickly as possible, I noticed

I was alone in the lobby. Nurse Bobbie was far away, attending to another patient.

I quickly reached into my bag and found my car keys. Standing slowly, I was encouraged to realize I was not too dizzy to walk. In moments, I was out the front door and in the parking lot. My heart raced as I saw my car, and the distance between the front of the clinic and my car was getting shorter and shorter. After opening the car door to the backseat, I gingerly eased in and locked the doors. Peering out my backseat window, I was relieved that no one was following me.

As soon as I lay down, my stomach started cramping. What felt like a tight knot in my stomach made me draw my knees to my chest as I tried to catch my breath, praying the cramps would subside. I kept breathing. Finally, the round of cramps lessened. One of the critical post-operative instructions, aside from the pain medication to have filled at the pharmacy, was to eat a full meal and drink fluids within a few hours of surgery. I had fasted since earlier that morning and was feeling hunger pangs as well as cramps.

I saw the late afternoon sun in the sky and wondered how long I might be lying in my car before Rick would come to take me home. The familiar feeling of abandonment settled upon me. Ever since Rick and I had gotten together, he'd encouraged me to cut off ties with all my family, even my new biological ones I had just recently met. I had no one to call. No one to reach out to.

These were some of the loneliest hours of my life.

Waiting for Rick. I didn't trust myself to drive. So, I waited. I tried not to cry since that seemed to make me contract my stomach muscles, bringing on another round of cramps. I asked myself why I didn't ask for help from the clinic. I still don't know why. I kept focused on waiting out the effects of post-surgery, waiting for Rick, and feeling more alone than I'd ever been.

I kept dozing on and off, waking occasionally, looking around, and then closing my eyes again. The discomfort was less if I tried to stay as still as possible.

However, after the cramps subsided, my core temperature must have dropped because I was shaking involuntarily with muscle spasms. The chills were unbearable, even though the California weather was a balmy 80°F. I huddled my body tighter, desperately trying to warm myself, both physically and emotionally.

At one point, I'd gathered enough strength to reach forward to turn on the car for the heat and to check the time. Before going to the clinic, I had removed my watch and other jewelry. The radio came on loudly, filling the inside of my car with a popular song by Michael Jackson, "You Are Not Alone." This made me cry again. Cranking the heat to as high as it would go, I discovered it was after 5:00 p.m. I'd been at the clinic since 1:00 p.m.

I dozed again and woke up to hear an insistent tap on the window from the other side of my car. Rick was pressing his face to the window to get my attention. It was dark, but I could make out that it was him. I was both ecstatic and furious. How different my life would have been if I hadn't opened my car door to him that day—or any other day.

"What are you doing in your car? Why didn't you wait inside the clinic?" Rick said as we both turned to look at the dark clinic, which had closed hours ago.

"Where have you been, Rick?" My tears of it all burst with the sadness and realization of the choice Rick and I had made that day and all that had been lost. The deep, hollowed-out feeling was crushing.

"I was in a major client meeting. I *couldn't* just leave! They wanted drinks after the presentation, which went exceedingly well, by the way! I came as soon as I could," Rick said unapologetically.

"Come on, let's go get something to eat. I'm starved." Rick's voice became soothing, "Come on, Emmie, I'll help you to my car. Why are you shaking? That's it. Take it real slow. I've got you. Everything's going to be all right. You'll always be my 'Lucky Emmie.'"

"Lucky Emmie" was a nickname Rick gave me when we first met. I represented youth and innocence to him, which he felt entitled to possess. Rick said it was proof that the universe gave him a second chance. But rather than using past mistakes to lead him to a purposeful transformation, he couldn't seem to do things any differently than he ever had. His overwhelming coping skill of blaming others for all his grievances echoed his proclivity to self-sabotage.

In hindsight, I realize how truly lost I was then and with that person. The justifications I made for thinking Rick was a safe and loving person for me are incomprehensible now. I often sit with my 24-year-old self, who felt she was in love and needed Rick to be the liberator he professed to be. Putting my arms around her, I hold space for the anguish of that fateful day at the clinic, as well as the 12 years I spent married to him. With a thankful heart, I tell her how proud I am that she shouldered the excruciating process of separating from Rick to protect herself and the two children she had with him after marriage.

The deprivation I experienced in my youth made me more susceptible to manipulators like Rick and Dr. Brenner, who made promises they never intended to keep. My inability to assess when someone is disingenuous has plagued me, but I'm grateful that's no longer true.

While I was able to "Drop the Rock," as a book from the Twelve-Step Program says, by asking my "Higher Power" to rid me of all my character defects and defenses, my children were still somewhat captivated by their dad when they were growing up. He used charisma and fantastical thinking to charm them until they, too, saw him clearly. After the divorce, Rick repeatedly proved that co-parenting with me was not part of his agenda. He made things as difficult for me as possible while he was the "fun" parent, occasionally taking them to movies or lunch. I still had to deal with him indirectly since he was the father of my children. They had lost so much after the divorce that I was adamant about supporting their relationship with their dad. But it was also true that I rid myself of feeling responsible for

Rick's actions or behaviors in any shape or form, albeit a tricky boundary for me to navigate.

My son recently asked me, "Is it my fate to end up like my Dad?"

Rick died before I was able to answer Trevor. I'll need to wait to answer until he's further processed his grief. He and his sister are overwhelmed by losing their father before turning 30. The fact that Rick and I were 20 years apart made a difference—especially since we had children who the generous gap would affect.

I want to share with Trevor, and I have experience with this, that we are not our parents unless we strive to be so. I believe in the power of choice and self-determination. I look forward to sharing with him that we, alone, get to define our identity and who we want to be.

So it is *not* with a heavy heart, other than for my children who never had the father they deserved, and the sadness I would have for anyone who chose to live the way he did, that I say one last goodbye: RIP, Rick Dorsey.

22

The Gate is Open

In my dream, I stand frozen before the rusted barbed-wire gate that ominously swings wide open. I can see through the low-lying clouds that The Gathering Place is just ahead upon the green grassy hill. It feels almost too good to be true, like a trap. My mind struggles to determine my next move. It seems logical to step outside the confines of the camp that has oppressed me for as long as I can remember. While I can almost visualize the neurons in my brain sending messages to my legs and feet, urging me to take the bold steps out of the prison camp, my body and mind feel disconnected. Sweat pools on my forehead and heavy drops roll down my cheeks and neck, even though the pleasant, warm early spring sun isn't to blame.

Suddenly, I face a newfound freedom. I slowly look down at my feet, reflecting on how strange it feels that they don't seem like my own. If they were mine, I could pick them up one at a time, moving forward. Instead, my legs and feet feel paralyzed, as if the tattered shoes I'm wearing are weighing me down by all the shock, deprivation, and anguish of my past. I close my eyes, gently commanding my mind to be still. The light spring breeze feels welcoming on my skin. I remind myself to take deep, full breaths to help calm me, and I hear my thoughts:

"You can trust this. You're free now. Are you willing to walk away from everything familiar that has been your enslavement, the bondage you consider as normal as waking up in the morning? If you choose, you could walk out of here right now. But if you can't start shedding the skin of who you used to be before that gate suddenly and miraculously stood wide open, you'll find yourself back here. The decision is yours."

Who am I now without the struggle and oppression? How will I define myself now and in the future? Is uncovering this scarier than remaining in the gilded cage I know so well? It's a state of being I've come to understand, with each wall of limitation firmly in place. There's no unexplored territory that eludes me within this confined space. I have always sensed the glue that has tethered me; all the while, I've tried to break free from its grip, leading to utter anguish and exhaustion. Pretending to escape became a dance, creating tension that stretched my life but always cruelly snapped me back. It was merely an illusion of freedom.

"So, what's different now?" I ask myself.

Silence. Nothing. I have no thoughts at all.

Then I hear the word *"choice"* as if from far away. It grows so loud in moments that it pounds, pulses, and reverberates—until I release it, rising from deep within me and escaping my lips.

I glance into the distance from my position at the open gate, feeling like I see another version of me waving from the edge of The Gathering Place. I look inviting, as though there is nowhere else I would rather be.

It's Satyana, my wise self. Her body appears strong, her face relaxed, and her eyes sparkle with life. She is gesturing to me to join the liberated, joyful version I've always been until I was coerced into forgetting my true self. Shaking my head back and forth from the open gate of the camp doesn't seem to deter Satyana from being a magnetic force pulling me closer. I suddenly hear Satyana singing a joyous melodic tune with lyrics expressing compassion, curiosity, clarity, creativity, calm, confidence, courage, and connectedness. The feeling the music provokes is intoxicating. Yet, still, I hesitate.

Fear and doubt, among other factors, diminish self-energy, curiosity, liberation, and equanimity. A spirit conditioned by a trauma bond develops a false and misguided loyalty to its oppressor. This raises the question: *What will it take to see things clearly and consistently? How can I make these discoveries my improved default setting?*

My answer is practice, reflection, dedication, and embracing the awareness that a new day has arrived. I've committed to fully living in this chapter of my life, refreshed with love, grace, and a dedication to authenticity. If I seek the truth, I must be devoted to it. I celebrate by carefully building a new foundation with flexible walls, replacing rigid ones. I'm practicing integration by saying "yes" to life while unapologetically setting healthy boundaries. I recognize that the beauty and complexity of everything are interconnected and that everything belongs. The catch is that everything can be embraced, but I can cling to nothing. Instead, the power is in letting things go. I embrace the paradoxes, the infinite joys, the unimaginable, and the heartbreakingly beautiful—and believe that they all have a place.

I ask myself, *What's the invitation?* I believe it's accepting the challenge and privilege of living in the mystery of being my full self—an invitation extended to us all. Aside from the gift of this life to live, it's an offer that comes without absolutes or certainties. We all get to choose how we experience it. The challenges, sorrows, and uncertainties come with the territory, as do the opportunities to love, dance, and be free.

Discovering freedom is very much like finding forgiveness. Both are fleeting, difficult to grasp, and often unsustainable. A more accurate description for each might be that they resemble shampoo bottle instructions—lather, rinse, repeat. Given the nature of change, this idea makes sense. The person I was ten years ago has evolved into a more genuine version of myself. To achieve this, I had to be willing to let go of the old story that I and others had created about me. A fresh perspective and ongoing personal growth enable me to reassess, reevaluate, rededicate, and update my system with new insights. One of my most cherished and protected values is to remember that change is essential for my expansion. So, I remind myself to forgive both myself and others and to recommit to freedom each day; it's a growth cycle I'm more than willing to repeat again.

As I stand today at the rusted, dilapidated iron gate hanging precariously from its hinges, I recognize the grace I grant myself when I admit that my work is far from finished. I still have more letting go to accomplish, and I accept that the renewal process is lifelong, just like finding forgiveness and claiming liberation. There's always something to release, and there's always something to learn. Even though the clouds above can appear ominous and untamable, I've learned to trust what cannot always be seen.

Because I believe these non-dualistic elements are interconnected in this vast universe, I can gently yet intentionally step through the open gate to follow my heart to The Gathering Place beyond. That's where a grand old oak tree stands, welcoming the chance to sink its roots deeper and broader into the reddish-brown earth with each passing day. The tree's limbs and branches reach and sway higher in the wind and sky, the wind helping to make it stronger.

If only for today, I will step beyond the ties that bind me, which I now recognize as self-imposed. I embrace the grace and promise of trying again tomorrow and the day after. Even amid the tears of it all, I intend to keep rising through the deep waters, choosing to breathe because it's medicinal. I cherish being present in this life to which we have all been graciously invited.

The End

About the Author

Emma Stevens, who is also known as Linda Pevac, is the author of two earlier memoirs: *The Gathering Place: An Adoptee's Story* and *A Fire Is Coming.*

Her adoption journey began when she was relinquished as an infant and adopted at three months old. Only in hindsight does she understand how being an adoptee has shaped and formed her entire life.

In her first memoir, *The Gathering Place*, Emma describes a magical space she has created for healing, comfort, and restoration for the younger parts of herself that never felt safe, seen, heard, or understood.

A *Fire Is Coming* is Emma's cautionary tale. She emphasizes the importance of selecting a therapist thoughtfully and alerts readers to the psychological nightmare that can result from an unethical therapist, doctor, or counselor.

Emma's third memoir, *Choosing to Breathe*, brings together all three themes. It takes readers back to The Gathering Place, where they discover what it means to integrate their identities as Emma releases multiple layers of trauma.

After graduating with a journalism degree from the University of Oklahoma, she pursued master's-level coursework in psychology at Pepperdine University in Orange County, California. In March 2024, Emma won an Independent Author Award for her second book, *A Fire Is Coming*, at Tucson's 2024 Festival of Books.

She was also a finalist in the 18th Annual National Indie Excellence Awards for the same book.

Emma loves traveling and spending time with her two adult children and her two lively, affectionate Bengal cats.

www.emmastevenswriter.com

Resources

Alcoholics Anonymous Twelve-Step Program: aa.org

The Enneagram (personality assessment tool): enneagraminstitute.com

Internal Family Systems (IFS): ifs-institute.com

Eye Movement Desensitization and Reprocessing (EMDR): emdria.org

Cognitive Behavioral Therapy (CBT): nacbt.org

Carl Jung's Concepts of True Self vs. False Self: cac.org

Nancy Verrier, *The Primal Wound*: a.co/d/2ivQ4pP

Betty Jean Lifton, Journey of the Adopted Self: a.co/d/3SgNVwp

The Adoptee Consciousness Model by JaeRan Kim, PhD: adopteeconsciousness.com

Richard Rohr's ideas on Order, Disorder, and Reorder: cac.org

Jesus' Sermon on the Mount discusses the themes of death and renewal. Refer to the New Testament, Gospel of Matthew, chapters 5, 6, and 7: biblestudytools.com.

Rob Bell, *Love Wins*: a.co/d/guaKmXK

Dr. Steven Hassan's BITE model: freedomofmind.com/cult-mind-control/bite-model-pdf-download/

Dante's journey through Hell, Purgatory, and Heaven in *The Divine Comedy*: en.wikipedia.org/wiki/Divine_Comedy

Spiral Dynamics is a model that outlines the evolutionary development of individuals, organizations, and societies: spiraldynamics.org/resources/books/

The Yogi's Journey to Complete Enlightenment: Self-Discovery and Spiritual Growth: yogainternational.com/article/view/exploring-the-eight-limbs-of-yoga-a-path-to-enlightenment

Abraham Maslow's Hierarchy of Needs: Self-Actualization: researchgate.net/publication/383241976_Maslow's_Hierarchy_of_Needs

The Seven Chakras: youtu.be/hhQC3blQkg4?si=WNe2UDPvbN_xiRSU

Erik Erikson's Stages of Psychosocial Development: simplypsychology.org/erik-erikson.html

Buddha's teachings on practicing Dharma and the Four Noble Truths: youtu.be/MbMatOLsK1s?si=lg7iZe8zL6xBdb3p

Ralph Waldo Emerson's teachings on Transcendentalism

inspire us to explore "our original relation to the universe": https://iep.utm.edu/ralph-waldo-emerson/

Joseph Campbell, *Hero's Journey*: jcf.org/learn/joseph-campbell-heros-journey

Maureen Murdock, *Heroine's Journey*: archive.org/details/heroinesjourney00murd

Eckhart Tolle's teachings on the power of presence and the awakened state of consciousness: The Art of Presence - Eckhart Tolle | A Guided Meditation

Rumi's poetry themes of overcoming fear and persevering through challenges: 7 Powerful Poems by Rumi - That Can Change Your Life

Anne Lamott, *Bird by Bird, and Somehow: Thoughts on Love*: a.co/d/hAf3lUL and a.co/d/cXXLQnh

James Nestor, *Breath: The New Science of a Lost Art*: a.co/d/8uzYDFJ

Gabor Maté, MD, and Daniel Maté, *The Myth of Normal: Trauma, Illness, and Healing in a Toxic Culture*: a.co/d/9M3Uuzy

Brené Brown, *The Power of Vulnerability: Authentication, Connection, and Courage*: a.co/d/36T3htZ

Scott Peck, *The Road Less Traveled*: a.co/d/cSwyG4x

Bessel van der Kolk, MD, *The Body Keeps The Score*: a.co/d/hNbuutR

Viktor Frankl, *Man's Search for Meaning*: a.co/d/6YcEhaR